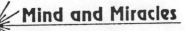

Mind and Miracles

16363 Cammi Lane
Fort Lauderdale, Florida 33326
(305) 389-8076

First printing April, 1988
Manufactured in the United States of America
Cover Design by Coleman Publishing

ISBN 0-87418-175-5

SPIRIT SPEAKS

MESSAGES TO A STUDENT
OF
"A COURSE IN MIRACLES"

TABLE OF CONTENTS

PREFACE

Dear Reader:

I am pleased that you have chosen to pass through this journal with me and Jana. It was meant to be that you chose to become one who shared this material. It was meant to be that the material herein was written just for you. Believe that, dear reader. This book will not fall into the hands of those who are on a different path, or into the hands of those who will become afraid by the reading of it, or into the hands of anyone who will seek to defy the Truth of which it speaks.

All who open their hearts will read it with their hearts, and the comfort that they seek will be theirs. Those who read it with their thinking minds will find some answers, some clarity of thought which will help them proceed through the "Course".

If your path is the "Course" do not for a moment think that this work is in any way a substitute for that study. No, indeed. If the "Course" is your path, stay true to it, keep studying it, trust it. Many writings will come which will help you in your learning. Accept them all as helpful. Remember that the real teacher is the Spirit which is already within your heart.

I bless you, dear reader, and give you my support and love as you journey on this plane. Remember that I speak to each one of you who will listen. I will speak to you through books such as this, or through the words of a friend, or through an experience, or directly through your own heart should you choose to open it.

Peace to you, my child.

The Voice For God,
Holy Spirit

INTRODUCTION -- PART I

December 8, 1987

I had been studying A COURSE IN MIRACLES for about two years, when a new element entered my work. One day, while I was reading a lesson in the text, an overwhelming urge came over me to pick up a pencil and write a letter to a dear brother who I knew was in pain. I resisted because I felt I had nothing wise to say to him. Yet the urge to write this letter was so driving that I could not resist it. So I gathered pencil and paper and began to write.

My letter began, "Dear Friend, I don't know what the hell I'm supposed to write, but I've been directed to compose this letter to you." As soon as the period was placed at the end of that first sentence, a flow of words poured through my pen, and as fast as I could write, words appeared on the paper as though my hand and arm were connected to some source outside myself. As I wrote, I realized that I had no idea about what was to come next. I recognized that my task was to relax and receive, to "Step back, and let Him lead the way," as it says in the Course.

The whole experience seemed preposterous, yet when I read the letter I had scribed, I knew that there was wisdom and comfort in it. I sent it on to the brother, with my love.

Throughout that day, I experienced many emotions. At one time I felt both honored and chosen, yet doubtful and skeptical. Then I decided to let the experience go, to turn it over to the Holy Spirit. In my next meditation, a clear message came from the Voice for God, (which I had become comfortable calling "Spirit"). The Voice said, "I will be asking you to scribe for Me -- to write down messages for yourself and others. Be prepared with writing tools." With that, my journey as a scribe for the Holy Spirit had begun. Now I share this experience with you.

THE SCRIBING BEGINS

September 1, 1987

Dear Child. I am pleased with your desire to join with me. I have watched you grow. I have watched you allow your love to reach out in fearlessness to your brothers. I come to you now to help you continue on your path, so that we may help move your world to its salvation.

When your heart is open, I will be there. I have chosen to communicate with you through the written word. You have already demonstrated your willingness to participate in this form of communion by scribing My words to one of your holy brothers when he was in need. I will continue to use you to be my scribe, to be attentive to my presence within you always so that I may speak clearly to you and others who want to hear.

When you are centered, when your heart is hungry for guidance, when a loved one needs my blessing, I will be there to speak to and through you. Our task is not a little one. Our work together will bless many people.

In the days to come, there will be words delivered to you to write down and study. Sometimes you will resist. Sometimes you will doubt the source. Sometimes you will question the content. But I know that as long as your heart is open to Me, the words and thoughts which come through you will be perfect for My purposes.

So, little one, together we have a mighty and challenging task. Let us get on with it . . .

COMFORT IS WITHIN

September 2, 1987

The comfort that you seek is within you -- it does not come from Me to you. It is in you. As you allow it to reveal itself to you, you will experience peace. My part is to keep you steady on the inner path. The world would pull you away to outer concerns. My voice reminds you that your focus needs to remain on the inner goal -- peace and happiness.

Peace and happiness are not of the body but are in thought and State of Mind. Prosperity is a way of thinking, it is not to be found in acquisitions.

When you feel separated you have chosen to worship at ego's altar -- and there I cannot come. When you need Me, and ask for Me, I will come. I cannot give you peace until you choose it by denying ego's claim.

Separation is an illusion, an alignment with ego. Loneliness is an illusion of the body. You are already joined in truth to all of the people in your life -- at the deepest level. Even those with whom you do battle are one with you beneath and beyond the earthly connection. You need but realize this to achieve peace with them.

Wish to see them sinless. A little willingness to practice non-judgement toward your brothers lightens ego's hold. I will erase the pain of supposed slights and mistreatments. A little willingness to see them sinless. Try it, my dear. You'll like it!

PRACTICE GIVING UP

September 7, 1987

It is all OK. Dismiss all melancholy. Remove all doubt. Return to Me in the place where I await you. Practice giving up -- turning over all which troubles you. No upset is too small. Every time peace is lost, look to the cause and turn it over to Me. Then look for the release from pain.

NO SEASONS

(Thinking about autumn with sadness ...)

September 7, 1987

Don't let the season diminish your growing. The world of spirit has no seasons. Only one -- that of Love. Be watchful not to let change on the earthly plane interfere with the real changelessness which is of Spirit.

SETTING THE PURPOSE

September 9, 1987

Beloved -- you come once again. The words that come are not startling, not unfamiliar, not surprising. But they do serve to focus you on your purpose.

Set the purpose before any activity. Set the purpose in each holy encounter. Do not debate the purpose for there is only One -- and what seem to be a million variations! But until that purpose is etched in your heart, continue to establish the goal, alone and with those like-minded.

Set the purpose before each "Miracles" class and ask the group to think about it silently. Setting the purpose each time will assure that you do not waste time in fruitless wandering.

Pray without ceasing.

Feel God's Words pour through your brothers as they speak to you.

Repeat God's words to yourself in the silence of your heart.

Allow God's Words to join you to Me.

Peace to you.

THE HOLY RELATIONSHIP

September 9, 1987

The holy relationship is a servant to my purpose. It is greater than you know. Your holy relationships are more powerful than you dream. They serve Me well, when fully turned over to Me.

The holy relationship is more than a human instrument. It is the extension of my love on earth. Your participation in it will bring that love into your life to fill all the corners you now perceive as empty. My love will bless each and every one you meet if you set the purpose thus. Allow My/Thy love to flow. Block it not, nor turn it off.

The holy relationship facilitates the flow of love to all people. The combined purpose of two people desiring to be channels of love will cause my light and love to reach the far corners of the earth. Your part in the plan for salvation is not small.

I say this to remind you of the grandeur of your commitment to me. I do not hold lightly, your desire to join Me. I remind you that our undertaking is vast, and your part is necessary. We are saving time for all in Our Union.

Keep on knowing that the holy relationship is the most perfect learning-teaching tool I can offer you. Remember that long ago, in a time which memory cannot recall, you chose the holy relationship as the means for returning home. All of your relationships are holy, when you have given them to Me. The Course in Miracles is a path of relationships. It is your path.

Concern yourself not about the means. I will clear the way. I will join with you as each obstacle appears. Stay in each moment. Be alert for ego's intrusion and give up the intrusion to Me. When doubt and fears arise, recognize that they are bringing to light the secrets which are still hidden. The hidden secrets hold the barriers between thee and Me. So welcome the fears -- they allow the light to penetrate where it has been blocked. Use the holy relationships when fears begin to overwhelm.

When your holy relationship brings pain or fear, you can be sure you have fallen back into specialness. Where specialness has entered, the ego is in charge, and ego's only purpose in relationships is to reinforce separation. When you feel disharmony in any of your relationships, turn over the conflict to Me. Ask for My help in giving up your sense of incompletion, so that I may teach you that you are already complete and so is the brother who shares with you the holy relationship.

This world honors only special relationships, those relationships built on the need to win, not lose; those relationships built upon the need to be completed by someone else; those relationships where neediness is the powerful motivator. A relationship is holy if either brother has made the choice to surrender the relationship to Me, knowing that loving and forgiving support the partnership, not competition or neediness.

Continue to re-dedicate all of your relationships to me. Every meeting is an opportunity to practice love and forgiveness. No relationship is insignificant. One brother's desire to commit a relationship to God is sufficient for the miracle of joining to happen. All relationships are opportunities for you to experience love and joy. All relationships are holy in the eyes of God. All you need do, is join with him in that commitment. Be willing to experience your innate holiness, my child.

The purpose of every holy relationship is to take you home. The purpose of the holy relationship is to serve as a model for all special relationships that they may be transformed into holiness. The purpose of the holy relationship is to provide you happiness on your journey home. The holy relationship will lead you into joy and peace, so that you may give joy and peace to your world. The purpose of the holy relationship is to teach you to devote yourself to My values, not the values of the world.

You have chosen the Path of Relationships, my child. Be at peace with that choice. It is the perfect choice for you. Your relationships will carry you home to the Father, who awaits you patiently. Peace to you.

SEE THE PERFECTION
September 12, 1987

My child, the power is within you. You CAN heal through your thoughts. Each time an unhealed condition, situation, or person comes to mind, heal them by knowing they are surrounded by God's holy love. Do not think about the disorder or disharmony. See only the perfection within.

It is important that you see this perfection with ever increasing strength, each time the problem comes to mind. Do not let your small mind dwell for one instant on the perceived problem. See instead the perfection of God's handiwork. How could lack of any kind exist in God's world? You are learning to see only God's world, not ego's world. Now meditate in peace. We will talk again later.

Peace -- my child.

OPEN THE HEART

September 13, 1987

Challenges are for growing through. God does not create them for you. The challenges come because of ego's desire to perpetuate the myth. The correction of the myth lies in your knowing, fearlessly, that the problem does not exist in God's reality, and that reality is the only reality. Pain and suffering are the ego's way of chaining you to the earth plane. Anyone who wholly wants God's peace can have it by being of My heart.

My heart is within yours -- hidden, yes, but available for the seeker who has the patience to penetrate through the ego's layers and layers of defenses. My heart and your heart are One. Come into your own heart. Leave at the door your thoughts, questions, answers, words and language. Simply knock on the door fearlessly and your heart which contains My own will open wide. All the comfort and release from pain and fear will shine out upon you. Admit your inability to understand, to solve your problems, to communicate your needs clearly. Admit all this. Admit you know nothing except that you are My Son.

As a son comes in humility to his Father, the Father will embrace him with all his love. So will I embrace you, my child, when you knock at the door of your heart. Let the thoughts, words, explanations, questions and all desires of your earthly mind go. All you need is to enter. The door is and always has been open.

Move into your heart in meditation. The journey is not long. The distance traveled will be eternity. I love you, my child. My heart and yours are already joined if you will but fearlessly open your heart to yourself.

The answers lie in your heart. Go there now. I am there and will meet you in peace. Go fearlessly into your heart. It will open and My heart will embrace you here, in the eternal Now.

Accept this message with your heart, not your mind. Accept this message with your heart open. Think only with your heart, my child. Rest your earthly mind. There is where the illusion of your fear exists. Inside your heart is purity and light and eternal safety. You are ready now to glimpse the brilliance of your open heart.

I await you there.

THE HOLY RELATIONSHIP

A Meditation

September 15, 1987

Mentally join for the purpose of focusing on the meditation.
Dedicate the meditation to the Holy Spirit.
Affirm the Oneness of all minds of the Sonship.
Affirm the One Mind of this Holy Relationship.
Express gratitude for the gift of this Holy Relationship.
Ask for guidance about fulfilling the purpose of this Holy Relationship.
Affirm that our hearts are listening and we choose God's Will.
Now I ask my Holy Brother to share his thoughts with me.
Affirm that my heart is listening and has heard the message.
Now I share my thoughts with my Holy Brother.
Affirm that I know my Brother has heard with his heart.
Choose the Peace of God for the relationship.

HOLY VALUES

September 18, 1987

God's values, not earth's values, are your goal, my child. Remember this well. My values encompass all values, and erase all inconsistencies of the world's values. Only Mine are whole. Partial values do not meet all needs. The values of the world are insufficient, small, limiting, fear-filled, confining, painful, inconsistent, and destructive.

My values are the order within Truth. They honor all honest efforts to return to Me. They are real, abiding, comforting, nurturing, loving, fully conscious, and peaceful. They connect, join, unite, enlighten, release, and bring freedom and laughter to the human heart. My values support love with unlimited devotion.

So, dear one, let go of the world, hold my hand. Come with Me. Come home. It is time.

THERE IS NO FAULT
September 20, 1987

Nothing is your fault. You are not at fault. The feelings of the people around you are not your responsibility. What IS your responsibility is to stay out of their feelings. Instead, nurture them with your love. In your extended love, no fear resides. If you feel fearful, you are not extending love.

Therefore, when things seem out of harmony, because those around you are in conflict, love them with openness and fearlessness. Your love cannot harm them or you. Leave the "fixing" to Me. I will intercede as allowed, but remember that you play an important part by preparing the way with your love of them.

Above all, do not allow their discontent to diminish your extension of love. Their discontent is a call for love. That is when the love is the most necessary. Think and act with your heart in those moments. Neither logic, nor arbitration, nor defensiveness, nor pacification will "fix" things. Keep your peace.

Ask *"What is the most loving thing I can do in this situation?" Ask, "How can I best show that I love and accept these folk?"* If that is your first concern, the matters about "What to do" will be resolved. It is in your need to know "What to do" that you experience fear and are paralyzed. In the "Being in your Place of Love with Them" the need to intervene will disappear.

Here is where "You need do nothing" applies. The acts of the body are insignificant. The devotion from the heart is all that truly matters.

Now, keep your peace. Extend love to all. Know that the Father has it all in hand -- in His hands. All is well. Truly, my child. All is Well.

Be peaceful now. Sleep the good sleep of the child of

God. I will be with you tonight. I will love you even in your dreams.

Peace, little one . . .

(This message came at a time when family conflict was great. I was feeling that my participation was fruitless, and I had lost my peace. Spirit reminded me that I am not the caretaker of my families'souls.)

EGO IS IMPERMANENT

September 22, 1987

To want each day to be holy is a goal to keep in your heart. When it doesn't seem to happen, keep on "keeping on." It is important to accept "down" days when inner exploration into the shadow places is happening just under your level of consciousness. Then when the shadows begin to rise to the surface light, you will be aware that spiritual work was going on even when you didn't feel it.

Protected you are, my child. The feelings that come and go, that provide mood swings and imbalance, are merely ego's expression of instability. Your true feelings are constant though not experienced all of the time. Your only true feeling is love, and it is the only constant in your life.

Just watch the feelings and give them no importance. Know as surely as the sun shines above that these superficial ego states will come and go. Permanence is not the rule. Expect change but do not invest any importance in it. As you unfold, you will spend more and more time in your only real emotion -- love. Until then, tolerate the changing aspect of earthly emotion with humor. Maintain your peace. Know with certainty that I am still working within you, that you will soon return to the real -- LOVE.

As I watch you work, I am joy filled. I see a dear child on her journey home. That pleases Me entirely. My need for you is as great as your need for Me. Completion requires all of us. The One misses the wandering thoughts and longs for their return. So when I see you on your return path, I rejoice.

I extend to you My comfort. I extend to you My strength. I extend to you My holy blessing. Ask for anything. I know your heart's desire and will join with you in finding it. Your heart's desire and Mine are One.

Peace to you. My love is yours. Share it willingly and joyfully.

YOU NEED DO NOTHING

September 26, 1987

It is all right. There is nothing amiss in the world. Once you fully realize this you will understand what "you need do nothing" means.

Your part, and this requires WORK, is to become mindful on a moment-to-moment basis of your Divine Connection to the Whole. It is when you lose this connection that the need to "do" (usually frantically) arises.

When in a Mindful State -- a state of remembering who you are -- the doing arises out of the moment. You will feel guided "to do," or you will feel free "to select a path or action" peacefully, or you will feel comfortable "not doing".

When you feel that where to put your foot next is a problem, then you can be sure that you have lost your Connection to Me. At that time, stop and re-commit, re-connect, re-establish your will with Mine. Then your foot will automatically fall, with naturalness and ease, in the correct place on the path.

Do not struggle. When faced with conflicting wishes, do nothing. Any decision made from a place of conflict will serve you ill. To wait will not harm you.

Child -- My path is not as difficult as you might imagine. You tend to make it so because in your past, good things seemed to come only as rewards after a long struggle. But that is an idea you were trained to develop. If you look more closely, you will see that where the real happiness was, effort was absent. Examine this proposition closely. See if it is not so. The real joy came as a flowing stream and swept you up with it. The happiness you think you "earned" was short lived and disappointing.

My Way is not a path of sacrificial duty. If you but open your eyes to the gifts that surround you, you will see this truth repeat itself again and again. For instance, your ability to teach well was not learned or earned -- it was My gift to you and it is through the use of that gift that you find joy. True? Sacrifice to duty did not earn you your teaching talents. The talent came freely.

You must work to keep clear about your ability through being mindful of being connected to the Source of the teachings. Staying connected takes diligence, not sacrifice. Through staying connected, the talent for teaching and learning expresses itself easily and naturally. That is because I want your talents to serve Me well. When your talents do not serve Me, struggle ensues. Is it not true?

By the way, work at developing greater trust for this instrument of communication. (The scribing.) If (as you sometimes fear) your ego disrupts or sabotages the thoughts, I will correct the error. You will become more skillful at recognizing the intervention of your ego. Then, fewer and fewer ego errors will happen. So relax, little one. Any errors will be automatically and painlessly corrected by Me!

(I continue to mistrust the validity of the scribing. Spirit keeps finding ways to remind me that ego would interrupt the flow of the words, and that I must keep an open mind and heart.)

ASK, THEN CHOOSE PEACE

October 1, 1987

You ask, *"How does it work? What shall I ask for? Should each act be brought before Spirit before it is done? Are there big issues to ask guidance about?-- Are their any issues too small to include in the request? If I ask and don't hear the answer, is it because Spirit isn't listening, or is it because I don't care, or is it because there are no right or wrong acts?"*

These questions are very complicated, I know, from your point of view. But from My point of view there is one simple guideline: If you are NOT SURE about a decision, ask. If you feel comfortable and non-conflicted, it isn't necessary, for your mind is now dedicated to aligning yourself with My Will. And when there is no conflict, your comfort in your feelings is your guide.

When there is conflict however, you need to ask. Now it is important to ask correctly. See the options you face and give them all up to me with the request for "What will bring me peace NOW?" That question I will answer. The answer may not come through a phrase or through the Voice. It may come through other means.

I know where your peace lies. You may not get the answer you want, but peace will still be in My answer. The behavioral act may not turn out the way you want, but the feeling of peace will be within you in spite of the unexpected turn of events.

Each time, after asking, reaffirm, "I choose peace". Then accept whatever happens as correct for your continued peace. Disregard whether or not the physical outcome was what you anticipated. You will receive peace, if you choose it after voicing your question. Ego will try to confuse you and say that if the outcome wasn't what you desired, then God wasn't listening. But that is not so. Peace can come in many ways, and many forms can deliver peace.

If you ask for guidance and choose peace about the request, peace will be yours, though not necessarily the outcome you desire. We will speak more about this dear one -- I know your struggle but it is unnecessary.

People make too much of being guided through the steps of doing and moving in the world. You are always being guided. You do not always choose to see the correctness of the guidance.

Continue to choose peace. Make that your mantra. Ask, "What would you have me do? I choose peace in the answer." Peace can be found in all answers. Your choice will always be correct if you choose peace -- after you ask for it.

MEDITATION

October 4, 1987

Meditate, my dear. These notes are not substitutes for the Quiet Mind. These notes help guide you while the learning is being consolidated. They help clarify the concepts and encourage you when you are down. But they do not take the place of your mental discipline.

The spiritual path does require practice. Perseverance in the practice of the presence, and vigilance in the watching of the thoughts is necessary.

What discourages you about your meditation is that there are no visible rewards. This worry is simply the ego's smoke screen. There are benefits and you know that! Think it through.

What you think you want are unusual experiences.

But you know in your heart that psychic experiences are not part of your path.

Be content, little one, to meditate without thrills and fancy packaging. Consistent practice in the quieting of the mind is all that is required. God does not have to prove Himself to you in order for you to know the importance of your meditation practice.

If you allow the meditation to cease, you will lose your connection to your truth. I am here with you. I am present in each meditation. I will strengthen your peace while you meditate, but you must put the body and mind in place before I can enter.

(I began to get carried away with the scribing and neglected my meditation practice.)

GOOD AND BAD -- NO DIFFERENCE

October 3, 1987

Ah, yes, dear child. Dissatisfaction now. Satisfaction earlier. They seem so different, yet they are the same. This morning was good. You were with God-connected people, teaching each other lovingly. But now, in inactivity, the mood is one of boredom and is unwelcome and uncomfortable.

It is all so unstable, these experiences of change. Humans seem to thrive on change, yet at the same time, are susceptible to illness and distress through too much change. All is so illusive.

In God's World of the One, change is impossible. Within you, dear soul, there is a place of changelessness. That is what the human heart yearns for - sometimes tearfully, always longingly. Changelessness.

Think about changelessness. How sweet it would be to be enfolded in the constancy of loving kindness. How nourishing it would be to be surrounded by the Father's arms. This is what the human heart yearns for -- rest from the fluctuations and mood swings of human happiness and sadness.

From this point of view, happiness is as responsible as sadness is for the discontent in the human heart. It seems a sweet reprieve, but being non-permanent, happiness contributes to the unsettling, because within the happiness is the certainty of its expiration to follow.

The happiness of God is not subject to swings, to highs and lows. The happiness of God is constancy. The happiness of God, for which there is no earthly word because the experience is unlike your human happiness, is one of no lack and therefore no fullness. In the happiness of God there is no wondering, no anticipation of the good, no expectation of pleasures to come, because you have it all in the One moment.

You in the human condition think you like pleasant surprises in the form of good luck, unexpected prosperity, and happy events. But the price for these "happy" human delights is that there must be an opposite -- bad luck, unpleasant events, bad news, deprivation and lack.

Are you ready to give up the "good" so you can give up the "bad"? The one is the price of the other. The one is at the cost of the other. If you would have My peace, you must be ready to see that the values of "good" and "bad" are the same. When you are ready to let go of the "good", peace will be yours.

Peace is constancy, comfort, communication, commitment, calmness. This is sweet, indeed. You see, the highs and lows of the human experience have no place in the Peace of Heaven.

When you realize you desire this and no other, it will be yours. As long as the "goods" are desired the "bads" will also be yours. (Actually, ego desires the "bads" as "good", for the "bads" reinforce it's power.) I ask you to choose My peace. This is what it means to finally see what is no longer of value -- to look at the human experience with a totally new perspective. Realize that the sadness of this life is yours only because you think you value the earthly joys.

I patiently await your return to heaven. I understand your reluctance to let go of what you think of as earthly joys. They do seem sweet. Yet the joys of heaven are sweeter still and I long for your return to them. I know that accepting the truth of this communication is difficult and will be met with resistance. It comes to you now because you are just now ready to begin to see the truth behind these words. To learn that there are no "goods" or "bads" too early, can be discouraging to the human spirit. I share this with you now because your progress has demonstrated to Me your willingness to listen with an open heart and not be frightened by the truths which I now share.

Long, long ago in earthly time, you agreed to accept this truth. The ancient memory listens and nods at the truth beneath the words and is satisfied. You are at a point in your progress where the memory of the sweetness of God's happiness brings a smile to your heart. When you can feel the heart smiling, my child, you know that the layers of shadows which hide the truth from you are slowly being pealed away. To give up the concept of earthly "good" will soon seem non-threatening to you. Only today were you ready to listen to this possibility without anger rising up in defiance and defense. Is it not true? Do you not smile now, even as these words are coming?

I will tell you when you can share these thoughts with others. Do not be aggressive about sharing. Be patient while I lead -- you follow. Peace to you, dear soul. You are indeed coming home. Yes? Yes!

TODAY IS A GOOD DAY

October 7, 1987

Today is a good day. All days are good days. All days are days for exploring the God within. All days are days for seeing the Christ in the world. This is the only way to look at "goodness" -- that which Christ is! So seek the good, seek the Christ -- which is another way of saying, "Know Thyself."

Some of you are experiencing various stages of negativity: despair, depression, doubt, disillusionment. These are all ways the ego brings you to damnation. Damnation, which includes all self-hate-filled thoughts and feelings, is the ego's final answer. Do you really choose to embrace damnation? Do you really want to walk into the darkness again where daylight is the miracle, where sunshine is unknown?

That is what you do if you give yourself to damnation, which is to give yourself to doubt, to despair, to depression, to disillusionment, and to denial of the Divine.

"But," you say, *"I have these feelings. I don't want them, I didn't invite them in. They came to me unbidden and they have stayed unwelcomed."* I say to you -- all your damning feelings have come to you at your choice, at your invitation. You have chosen ego's blessing, not My own. The ego would like to destroy you and so has called upon these "guests" to see to your destruction.

But you sometimes forget that there is a Holy Spirit standing by to help if only you would ask. The Holy Spirit can take these feelings and transform them to love and peace. He can look at doubt in a new way, and use doubt to bring to light that which is in confusion. He can look at despair and bring to light the hidden pain your little child still feels. He can look at depression and help you see that depression clears the way to inspiration. He can take disil-

25

lusionment and make you see that the real illusion is that which you call "reality". He can see denial as the refusal to give power to the unreal world of form.

There is no darkness the Holy Spirit cannot light. There is no human experience which the Holy Spirit cannot turn to spiritual fulfillment. Just as you have chosen to play in the ego's damnation, you can choose to play in Spirit's delights. But choose you must. The choice is entirely yours, not Spirit's and not even ego's. The "you" behind the ego illusion must choose to renew your commitment to the Real, to your Divine Connection. Turn all the damning, destructive pain over to Spirit, to Me, my child.

The only reason that you cling to this pain is that some part of you yet unrevealed, still in the darkness, desires the pain which it interprets as human pleasure. Admit to yourself that there are parts of you still unbidden to enter the light which would rule your destiny. Then invite those hidden secret parts into the light where they can be loved, where they can be released, where they can be healed. Surrender to Me all of the hidden thoughts and memories. Surrender to Me all of the misunderstood, unacknowledged, frightened step-children still hiding within the shadows of your heart. It is these vulnerable step children the ego uses to distort your wishes, and use them again and again he will until they are coaxed lovingly out into the sunshine of the Father's love.

Go within and call to them lovingly. Be not afraid of their re-appearance. Gently urge them into the light of God, that the ego's deceitful use of them may be stopped. Old memories, long forgotten fears, ancient histories of imagined heresies will come forth and be transformed into sparkling bits of light, into whose presence despair and depression cannot enter.

None of the pain you now experience need interfere with your progress. I will take each tear, each sigh, each heart-ache, each uncertainty, each stab of remorse and use it to light your path. The darkness shall be made light.

The choice is before you, and you will make it again and again: stay in the darkness of ego's damnation, or choose the light and watch the horrors become transformed into delight.

You are not failing. You are not failures.

I have seen your desire to work with Me. I am beside you even now when you feel abandoned. I have not left you.

You have turned your gaze away from Me and cannot see Me. The tears in your eyes blur clear vision of Me. You have closed your eyes in fearfulness of ego's mad threats.

BUT I AM STILL HERE waiting for you to turn your head and look upon Me. When you do this, your eyes will open wide, the tears will disappear, and all will be made clear.

(This message came to A Course in Miracles study group at a time when many members were feeling frustrated and experiencing doubt. It was the first time I felt compelled to share with my fellow students that Spirit was communicating with me in this way.)

THE EARTH -- A SCHOOLROOM

October 7, 1987

The learning escalates. The challenges multiply. Gradually the challenges which used to bring frustration and confusion, now bring simple affirmation of the truth. Where before you would dread earthly discomforts, now you see in them the possibility of unlimited personal growth. And you realize I am with you each and every step -- available to help you say and do the peaceful thing as needed. When a fear arises now, it is simply a reminder to turn inward, it is a call to Me for help. As soon as the fear is turned over the debilitating affects are gone and peace returns.

As you grow you begin to see this earth plane merely as the schoolroom in which to master the curriculum you have chosen. This earth plane is no longer a place from which to escape. You used to want heaven in order to escape earth's pains. Now you seek heaven because it is the place to fully know God. And heaven is not a place but a state of mind that accompanies the sweet yearning for union with God. I say "sweet yearning" because the desire to be with God is no longer a headlong scramble to get away from the demons. The yearning is instead, the gentle, comforting knowledge that you are yielding into the Divine. You are melting into the One. You are flowing with the stream and the only possible destination is the Universal Ocean -- your inevitable home.

There is a calm place in your heart where you can return when the "forms" become difficult. You now know that your heart's desire is indeed Mine. You still do not know how to stay out of the "forms," but then that is why you are on earth: to learn to be with the "forms" and not "of" them. And this learning is indeed happening.

My peace is yours. The love you practice multiplies

and extends outward. You are fulfilling the function I set for you during that ancient moment when the thoughts in the Mind of God seemed to separate. The world becomes a holy place as holy instants multiply. Believe that I will continue to make the way smooth. I will continue to guide you home. Peace, to you, dear one.

WHEN PEACE LEAVES

October 9, 1987

Peace to you my child. Rest in the knowledge that all is well. When peace leaves, know that it is only temporary. Sometimes peace comes and goes for a specific reason and your higher self will use those times to make you aware of your choices. When peace suddenly evaporates, use that to help you look for imbalance, for in the imbalance is the error. Correct the imbalance and peace will return.

Earthly pleasures will help or hinder depending on what they are used for. Remember to ask, "What is this for?" each time a new situation presents itself. Then the way will be smooth.

THE PRACTICE

October 12, 1987

Don't neglect your practice, even though emotions are tangled. This is the time for even greater persistence. Be strong in your meditation practice, in setting your purpose, in listening to your inner guidance.

If you feel blocked open yourself to Me. Come and say, "Please guide! I am listening." And I will answer -- if not through the Voice or scribing, I will find another way. I will reach you even in times of great trouble.

You see my child, I need you to complete your part in the plan. You are so dear to Me. Your gifts are needed for the Atonement.

What's happening now is difficult only if you forget your center. Ask, "What is the loving thing for me to say, to do?" I will lead you to the answer. There is reason in the drama. You need to look at it through My eyes. Where you don't understand, ego has intervened, and it doesn't matter because as you turn over to Me all confusion and fear, I will correct it perfectly.

I am here, my child. I am watching the drama. I will correct all errors upon your invitation!

Peace, dear soul, peace.

THE QUIET MIND

October 13, 1987

The Quiet Mind, the Quiet Heart, the Quiet Center -- all lead homeward to God. Frantic thoughts, fearful feelings, failures in the world of form, all lead to pain, disillusionment, and separation from God.

Your earthly work is to cultivate the Quiet Mind. Within the Quiet Mind all is peace and beauty, all is peaceful and beautiful. When the world overwhelms you with confusion and fearful possibilities, remind yourself to return to the Quiet Mind.

In the Quiet Mind, the Quiet Heart, I await. There I will greet you with the comfort a Father gives to his frightened, lost child. There you will remember that you only dream. In the Quiet Mind, the dream stops and reality is yours. In the Quiet Mind all forms of worldly attachment fall away and expose the illusion for what it is: empty wonderings, empty wanderings. Cultivate the Quiet Mind.

Determine to spend time with Me daily, communicating without words. Ignore the thoughts, they merely decorate the dream. The thoughts do not interfere with My communication with you if you give the thoughts no mind. The Quiet Mind lives even within the thoughts. Thoughts are not powerful enough to block the wordless messages I share with My children. Worry not about the thoughts.

Just sit with the quiet resolution that you desire God's blessing and guidance. That is enough. My wordless message will be there. You will feel its impact.

When you feel busy and distracted and unable to become still, even then you may come into your Quiet Mind, for I am within and can cut through the busyness if you are willing for Me to do so.

My child, to attain peace requires only a commitment, not sainthood. Bring your desire to connect with Me to Me, even when you feel very disconnected. If it is in your will to meet with Me, I can reach through the busyness of the outer mind and draw you into the Quiet Mind.

There I will whisper to you and you will know. Reality is in the Quiet Mind, not in the world. And the world, however much it may beckon to you to become immersed in its drama, cannot destroy your reality which is in your Quiet Mind.

Take the time to come to Me, to call to Me, and I will bring you in. You do not need to have a quiet mind to find Me. You need only desire to walk into your Quiet Mind to find me.

Spectacular experiences are not the goal. The inner smile of recognition is enough. Your reward will be in knowing we have touched -- you and I -- and My silent message will be received and demonstrated in your life.

THE HEART

October 13, 1987

The heart of the mind is within the heart,
*   not in the mind.*
The center of the heart is in the mind.
The mind is in the center of the heart.
Find it so.

The space within the heart
*   is where the quiet mind lives.*
The quiet mind is the Self,
*   stripped of the world's impositions.*
The unadorned "I" is in the space within the heart.
Father, help me find it.
Help me find it so.

My mind thinks it thinks.
My mind thinks thoughts, it thinks.
But thinking is not real.
Reality is total thoughtlessness,
*   total absence of thought.*
Reality is not what the mind thinks it is,
*   for the mind that thinks thought,*
*   is not real.*

The real mind is the space within the heart.
The quiet mind.
It does not think.
It KNOWS.

Father, help me find it.
Help me find it so.

THANKSGIVING

October 13, 1987

My gratitude abounds.
Thank you, Father.
Thank you for the gifts freely given.
Thank you, Father.

Thank you, Father, that I can begin to see gifts
in human pain . . .
That I can begin to see joy
within unhappiness . . .
That I can begin to see hope
in hopelessness.

Thank you Father for the opening of the Heart.
Thank you Father for the opening of the Quiet Mind.
Thank you Father for the desire to know the Truth.

Thy Will Be Done.
My Will Be Thine.

Words point towards --
but do not reach.
Thank you for the experience of
reaching, arriving, finding.

That is the Holy Instant,
An instant out of time.

YOU ARE LOVED

October 15, 1987

You are loved by the Father and His children. You are needed for the completion of the Atonement. When sadness interferes with your work on My behalf, I too am saddened. Then I long to hold you and ease your sorrow away. I long to talk to you and remind you of your greatness, of your gentleness, of your kindliness, of your loving presence. I long to remind you that you are the Son of the Father and as such, you are exactly like the Father.

The only thing you lack is that you don't know you are the perfect Son of the perfect Father. A small, insignificant part of you has convinced you that you can know lack. A small insignificant part of you has convinced you of its supremacy and robbed you of the conviction of who you really are. A small insignificant part of you has convinced you that you are unloved. In truth, the only love you lack right now, is that of yourself for yourself.

And so I come to remind you to let go of the insignificant thought that you are limited by pain and sorrow. Do not allow the tiny flea-sized doubt to master the whole flock, and cause such confusion among the many that all order is lost. Treat the tiny flea as the minute irritant that it is, no more significant than a tiny candle is when held against the sun's glowing radiance.

You, my child, are a beautiful thought which reflects your Creator. See your majesty, not your littleness. Believe that the Father loves you. Learn from that perfect example, that you deserve your own love. Your own love of yourself is the only thing that you lack, all else is already yours. Hear this gentle reminder, child. Be as loving to yourself as you are to me. Permit no self inflicted harshness to tarnish the truth about yourself. When you have learned to love yourself perfectly, this journey on earth will be over. Time will stop for you and We will be One ~~ain in heaven.

36

LONELINESS

October 15, 1987

There is a peace to behold in loneliness. Loneliness reminds you that you are not yet at home. Loneliness remind you that separation is not your natural state. Loneliness compels you to correct the error and return to your holy home of Oneness.

Within Oneness your loneliness cannot exist because One cannot want for anything. One is complete within itself. It is only where there are two that lack of union can exist. So see the loneliness as a witness that you are beginning to remember the Truth -- which is that you are One, not one among many, but One with the many: joined, unseparated, whole, and complete.

Ego would have you view loneliness differently. Ego would have you see loneliness as proof that two cannot join in peace. There is always a feeling of separation, even when love seems real. There is always the fear that the other will leave, or fail to return. That loneliness the ego uses to reinforce your "fear to love". But ego does not see with open eyes. And ego would mislead you and have you hate the other for failing to complete your emptiness.

Choose which way to see loneliness, Ego's way or My way. Then, having chosen the correct way to view loneliness, turn it over to Me, my child. Turn it over to me whenever it reappears so that I may use it to remind another brother that he is awakening to his natural desire to join.

Keep learning and keep loving. Your heart is open. The path before you is wide and clear. When you can see obstacles, such as feelings of loneliness, as opportunities to practice turning over the dream to Me, then the Peace of God is close at hand.

I am always with you. No loneliness is great enough to dispel My love for you. Truth may be obscured by the ego, but never, never destroyed.

37

STAY HEALED

October 17, 1987

"What more should I do? What more can I do?" you ask. If love has been extended, if the willingness to be healed and to heal has been extended, it has been done. There is no more to do.

But you must keep your heart and mind extending the love, and extending the healing moment to moment. Do not withdraw thinking, "Well, I did all I could. Now I can withdraw, my duty performed, the necessary steps taken." No indeed, the continuation of the extension of the love, and the continued willingness to be healed must be your choice now and now and now.

Be not discouraged if the offered healing seems not to have been accepted. It has been received, even if not accepted yet. If you allow yourself to doubt that the gift has been truly received, you dismiss your own healing. Healed you are, but in order to experience the affects of the healing, you can entertain no doubt. If you doubt, you will yet again sink into your own imagined unhealed state of mind.

Stay healed my child. Turn over the doubts and fears about misplaced or misunderstood healing to Me. Because your effort to heal and be healed came from the heart, healed you are. Stay confident of that. Leave the rest to Me. As more needs to be done, you will be directed.

If you resist My reassurance that all is well, your ego is in charge -- know that with certainty. Ego is always at the helm when you feel threatened, or attacked, or in pain. That is true even when the pain you feel is someone else's. Being a martyr is in not God's plan for you. Martyrdom is always ego's plan. Learn to recognize that, my child, and you will begin to let go of your need to play the martyr.

I say all of this to reassure you of what you already

know. So far you have accepted the truth of this with your intellect only. As the learning reaches the heart, the truth is fully realized and then finally experienced.

I know it seems difficult. That is because you share your brothers' pain. You allowed their desperation to color your own attitude. You need not do that. Keep true to yourself. Ignore the apparent ugliness around you. Remember, in forgiveness the thought is, "It never happened".

Each time you meet the other, let go of the last encounter and allow the new encounter to be unclouded by memory. If you do this religiously you can maintain your peaceful perspective. It takes only a little willingness and practice. Then open the eyes to see the witnesses to the truth of what I say.

Above all, remember I am with you. Everyone is working through their misperceptions in order to get to the truth. You cannot delay their progress - only your own. Keep on sending love. Keep on being healed. God's laws are forever operating even when you don't see them. One day when all the obstacles to love are removed, you will experience the brilliance of the Father's Love. You will join with your holy brothers in the warmest union possible. This will all be in a space/place which is beyond words, beyond language, and beyond earthly thought.

Keep on dear child. Look for the witnesses to keep you clear. Remind yourself to withdraw from ego's dance and join the Father in His magnificant symphony of color and sound and light which is Joy.

My peace to you, blessed one

HOLD NO PAINFUL THOUGHTS

October 18, 1987

Decide today to choose not to hold on to any painful thoughts. As soon as you recognize that you are sinking into a pain filled reverie, choose to turn it over to Me. This will take diligence regarding your thoughts. That is what your years of meditation practice have been for -- practicing mindfulness, watchfulness, and awareness of the mind's activities.

Let no painful thought linger once you have recognized its presence in your mind. Turn it over. If it or a related thought returns, turn it over again and again, until the unwanted thought disappears.

This will speak to the ego forcefully, telling ego that you will not tolerate its intrusion into your peace for one moment after your awareness is awakened. It matters not how many times you need to repeat the process. The act of repetition will teach your ego of the seriousness of your determination to return to God. The ego will therefore be weakened as you withdraw its fuel, and it will retreat, exhausted.

In this way, you can see how painful thoughts can be transformed by you and Me together into a tool for denying the illusion, a tool for supporting the truth.

Let Me remind you -- there is nothing dark enough, painful enough, shameful enough, or fearful enough to withstand the transforming power of Spirit. The pain of this world cannot but be turned into light. All that the ego makes -- no matter how clever, or sinister, as convoluted, or distorted, or dishonest, or deceitful it may be -- can nevertheless be transformed into a gift for heaven by Me.

So go ahead and see the difficulties of the dream. Experience them as much or as little as you choose, but then always turn the feelings of doubt, confusion, pain, and hopelessness over to Me. Reality, which I represent, will transform all illusions back into itself, and love will grow out of the ashes of your despair. How can evil possibly win? It doesn't even exist. This you will experience as you awaken from the dream.

CHANGELESSNESS

October 18, 1987

It seems you humans flirt with ego pain, then move to the Father's Love, then return to ego again. This changeability is an appearance only because the true Self is already securely in the loving arms of God. The times you spend doubting, being "of the world", being captured in the earthly illusion, merely delay your journey home.

These delays are occasions of learning also. Just look at the feelings that come up when you experience the world as a hostile and warlike place. Experience them as fully as you desire, hang on to them for as long as you please, enjoy the anger or sorrow or pain that these earthly connections inspire, but realize that the fall into pain is not permanent. For things of the ego are impermanent and changeable.

It is only the things of the Spirit that are permanent -- this you know. Only God's experiences are constant and unchanging. Therefore treat your thoughts about disaster and ruin and despair, as you would treat a bad head cold. The cold will go away, the miseries that it brings will leave, and you will enjoy your health all the more for its absence. So with your depression. It will go away because it is of the ego. And when it lifts, you will treasure your connection to God all the more. His arms will feel more strong and more loving, more comforting and more permanent than ever before.

So, walk through your despair remembering that despair cannot last, it is impermanent by nature.

This you have come to believe, yes? Let this understanding comfort you until the time you choose to walk back into the Father's arms. There are lessons to be learned in depression, it is sure. Learn then as quickly as you will. Then, when you tire of the struggle to understand, turn over to me what remains unresolved and I will lift you back into your true home, which is heaven.

Peace to you dear soul. I am with you now. I assure you peace is permanent, your forgetting to experience your peace is temporary.

KEEP ON
October 22, 1987

Let not discouragement close the heart. You tend to give up easily, a childhood trait. You lean towards quitting as an affirmation that, "Nothing matters, anyway." But now you know that it ALL matters in terms of allowing God's love to touch every aspect of your life.

Quitting locks God outside. Quitting reinforces ego's stronghold. Now is not the time for apathy. Now is the time for renewed willingness.

All I ask for is willingness. You can give Me that much, my child, even when you are disabled by self pity, and blinded by ego darkness. Your little willingness, and My love for you together are strong enough to bring light to a whole continent. Stay with Me. I will not turn away. Don't let go of Me, dear child.

THE MAGNET

October 23, 1987

You believe that if you could just be alone, and not be bothered by anyone else, you would be happy. You mind your business and everything seems pleasant, under control, and even peaceful. Then suddenly, someone intrudes upon your peace by surrounding you with his unhappiness. Like a magnet, you have drawn out of someone else his pain and disharmony, and now it is your burden. Now not only do you have his pain to bear, but you have also accepted the burden of feeling bitter towards the person who "shared" his pain with you. Twice blessed !! Yes?

But what really happens when you "catch" someone else's pain, is that, any matching pain which is already within you, is merely drawn up to the surface where you can look at it, experience it, and then discard it by turning it over to Me.

Therefore through Spirit's eyes, it can be seen that your brother has given you a gift -- he has encouraged the hidden step-children of misery to rise to the light where they can be seen as unloved aspects of yourself.

Then the healing can be invited in. My child, do not despair even when in despair! Do not reject even when feeling rejected. Do not withdraw even when you feel abandoned. Do not become hopeless even when you feel hopeless.

All of this can be used to open, instead of, to close the heart. Allow Me in to work the transformation. Allow Me in to soften the hard edges of pain. Allow Me in to offer you a different point of view. Allow Me in to kiss the hurt and pain away.

So many ways to look at feelings. Choose My way, dear child. Then peace will follow.

INSANITY

October 23, 1987

Again comes unhappiness, apathy, despondency, apprehension appear; another round of fear and guilt and pain. The human dilemma again and again.

One uncomfortable feeling is no better or worse than any other. They are all the same. Ego would have you pay more attention to one than the other because earth's values have taught you that despair is worse than despondency, hate is worse than dislike, anguish is worse than sadness. But I remind you, they are all equally insane -- yes, insane. Treat them as ego insanities. Turn then over to Me.

If you permit the negative feelings to linger, they send down roots in the ego's sandy soil and cling fiercely. But no matter how deep the roots, sand cannot hold them permanently, the release must come sooner or later.

These unhappy feelings are not harmful if you do not embrace them. Remember, they are impermanent as are all of ego's effects. Walk through them peacefully. Turn them over again and again and again to Spirit.

You are not fighting a losing battle. The battle is already won. The ego has already vanished and you are already in the loving hands of your Father. Heaven is already here.

Be alert to how quickly, even fleeting moment of sadness drag you down. In a flash, a bright day turns cloudy, a pleasant experience dissolves into gloom. Even passing thoughts are like great, opaque clouds drawn across your view.

Your work is to identify the first stirrings of the disabling feelings. As soon as you recognize the intrusion, give notice to the ego that you are aware of his game and will not play. Then turn over that which is not of value to

Me, and walk through the experience peacefully. I will walk beside you, My child. am always walking beside you. I will hold your hand if you but reach for mine.

STAY CENTERED

October 24, 1987

Stay centered, my child. Help your holy brother stay centered. Participate not in his drama, except as a brother who sees his friend in a bad dream. Wake him from the dream lovingly. Reassure him of your constancy. Offer him God's holy blessing again, and again, and again. You contribute to his suffering if you allow yourself to fall into fear.

Give your fear to Me, thereby helping to keep yourself sane. You cannot know exactly what is going on but you know that it is unreal. Affirm that nothing unreal exists. Affirm for your holy brother that nothing which is unreal can possibly affect him. Nothing that is unreal can affect the holy relationship. Then turn over all that is unreal in the holy relationship to Me.

Do this for him through the gift of the holy relationship. Herein lies the blessing of the holy relationship for you both. Your sanity is his. His insanity is yours to turn over.

Peace, dear child.

REACT NOT

October 25, 1987

You are loved. I am standing by you when ego attacks. Remain defenseless even in ego battle. If he has nothing to fight, the battle will dissipate because action needs reaction to sustain itself.

> Analyzing is "reacting".
> Anger is "reacting".
> Even retreat is "reacting".

When insanity reigns:

> Return to My arms and turn over each and every need to react you can uncover. Seek and find and release. That is all. Do not engage in the battle.

In My heart is safety on the battlefield. Come in.

THE HEALED CAN BUT HEAL

October 27, 1987

The healed can but heal. Extend your healing now by seeing in the world God's holy imprint, by seeing in the world God's holy purpose behind every event, by seeing in the world God's blessings enfolding each living thing.

Being healed, you are blessed and can see clearly through Spirit's eyes, and the world you see is heaven. This is the only moment there is. This is the only truth there is. Be in joy that it is given you to see thus.

This moment will last a lifetime, for every moment is a lifetime. Share with your holy brother your experience of grace for it belongs to him too. He will experience the holy healing because you will him healed with you.

The healed can but heal. You have received the healing, now accept it.

CHOOSE PEACE
October 27, 1987

If you see a situation where peace is not, and you desire peace there, work on bringing peace to it. If you are aware of any relationship in which you are withholding love, ask for help to open your heart to that person. If you see where work needs to be done, do it.

The work is in the mind, remember. You do not have to stay close to the problem to heal and be healed. You can stay close to the problem and I will help you. Or you can place distance between yourself and the problem, and I will still help you.

Work on letting go of whatever you feel interferes with your peace. Healing relationships brings peace. Making changes in the world of form can help bring peace also. But being unforgiving, dishonest, or trusting not does not bring peace.

To move or not to move is irrelevant. You choose either course -- they are equally correct, or not correct. What matters is teaching love through whatever choice you make. It is necessary to build peace with your brothers. The time you select to build the peace is also irrelevant, it matters not whether you are near them or not. If your desire is to choose peace, it will be accomplished.

Under My guidance, the lessons will be designed. Whatever adjustment in the world of form you select, I will still present the appropriate curriculum. I do not approve or disapprove of worldly decisions. I do not require anything as preparation for "the next step". Go ahead and take whatever step you desire, whatever step you feel will bring you closer to peace right now. The appropriate lessons will be there.

Staying stuck in the world of form by thinking that worldly attachments matter, does not bring peace. Use the world of form to practice communicating love, that is all. You can't use it to run away from your function. That is impossible for the curriculum will find you wherever you go.

So concern yourself not about My plan for you. My plan will demonstrate itself through the lessons I arrange. These lessons will be played out in your mind. You do not have to be in the right place or time, or have the right mental attitude to receive the lessons. The lessons are always perfect. The forms do not interfere with the lessons. I find opportunity in all of your situations.

So go about your life seeking peace in whatever seems the most reasonable way to you. Do not concern yourself about leaving lessons unlearned or unfinished. That is impossible. All lessons will be completed.

You have chosen to join with My Will which is your will. You have given yourself to Me, to be a Teacher of God. Do you think that I would let a Teacher of God get lost in the world of form? Do you think that I would allow a Teacher of God to be limited by the world of form? Do you think that the world of form matters at all?

Do not waste precious time debating simple earthly decisions. Choose peace again and again in whatever seems to be the most reasonable way at the time. Then act on that decision. Do not second guess and cloud up the waters. With an open heart, and the desire to choose peace, there can be no error.

Peace to you my child.

LOVING

October 29, 1987

Loving, any kind of loving, brings remembrance of the Truth. No matter how incomplete, how imperfect, how misguided, or how misunderstood it is, any attempt to be loving is pleasing to the Father who accepts all attempts at loving as complete.

So, dear child, do not fault yourself if you feel that your love isn't perfect. Do not fault yourself if you feel your love isn't a perfect reflection of Divine, unconditional love. You ARE perfect love in Reality. Your play in love in the world of form, can but bring the experience of God's Love into the planet's awareness.

LET LOVE IN

October 29, 1987

We are all the same, my holy brothers, you and I. We are joined, and we are One. The truth is True.

Our egos strive to separate us -- and love attempts to heal the separation. When we feel the wonderful flow of love, we begin to remember what oneness feels like. The memory is sweet, but dim. Love is what walks the earth in perfect grace. It has been given us in perfect trust to use to open the heart's memory to our reality.

Letting the love in, is our task, and it is our hope, and it is our fear. Ego teaches there is scarcity in love, that it comes in a finite amount and can be wasted, or lost, or stolen. But this is not so.

Love is unlimited. It multiplies as it is given. It expands when you accept it. Love cannot be diminished. Therefore, accept each moment of love that is extended to you. Each moment will become an hour. Each hour will become an eternity. And all of the Universe will be blessed.

Then extend your love freely back to your brothers, and it will multiply so that even the tiniest, most fearful of hearts will be showered with love. Even the tiniest most fearful of hearts will bloom.

The truth is True.

INTO SPECIALNESS

October 30, 1987

Yes, my child, you have been experiencing the pull away from the holy relationship. The pull away is the return to specialness. As joy slipped away, the specialness returned with confusion, uncertainty, guilt, and sorrow. Due to losing the NOW, the resulting flight into future preoccupations slammed you into a brick wall of total separation, total specialness. Then did you plunge into listlessness, sadness, apathy, doubt, and fear. Reread your work. It's all about depression and despair and mood swings and change -- endless change. Is this not the hallmark of specialness?

Your future fears are all a part of the specialness state, too. When contentment is present, the future disappears, and with it all the worry and distraction that goes with looking at the world through ego's eyes. Only ego lives in the future. I have recently reminded you of that!

To return to holiness now, ask yourself about your willingness to experience love as I would have you experience it. I remind you, there will be no loss. You will experience a return into your ancient memory in which the blessings of love are peace and contentment. Are you willing for this step inward? It is a giant step -- one not to be feared but embraced. This step will bond your holy relationship to Me and I will make you My angels to serve all of God's children through the love we share. Do you want this my child? Ask yourself.

"Yes, Holy Spirit, I do want to see. I do want to be willing to receive with gladness your plan for me. I do want to let go of the old ego values and experience the values of Spirit. I believe in non-scarcity of love. I believe that there is no call in God's plan for sacrifice. I accept God's happiness for myself now. Take me home, Holy Spirit. I am willing."

Then, dear soul, it is done for you as it is done for your holy brother. Our commitment is holy and specialness will no longer blind you.

I will use your flirtation with specialness to remind you of your commitment to Me. Then the specialness will serve us all, and keep you clear and focused and centered. Each lapse away from centeredness will bring enough discomfort to remind you of the sweetness of the Father's Love. Then discomfort will be seen as a holy tool, not an unholy punishment.

Peace to you, dear soul. Each step you take breaks down the barriers to love, and each barrier that falls will make the journey more peaceful. Hold Me in your heart. You are already within Mine.

(This message came at a time when a relationship which had been running smoothly, suddenly became full of uneasiness and suspicion. Spirit reminded me that maintaining a holy relationship takes constant work and application of love and forgiveness.)

SANITY IS REAL

October 30, 1987

Insane you can never be. Insanity belongs to the world of form, ego's kingdom, which is illusion. Yes, you can suffer from the illusion of insanity, but that has already been your life's whole experience. To invite "a little more" insanity, then? Is there "more" or "less" insanity, or is there just sanity and insanity?

Fear not the insane ravings of the ego, dear brother. You could no more become insane than I, for we are One, are we not?

And you have joined with Me in the Holy Kingdom of Consciousness which leads to Heaven on earth. Your conscious choice to see this world through My unclouded view, makes total insanity forevermore impossible and unreal. And a part of your mind knows and clings to that knowing, even when ego seems to have snatched your very soul away from Me.

The part of you that knows, needs but to whisper to the insanity, of sanity's holy presence, and the insanity will melt away like snow in bright sunlight.

Remember this, you are saved already. Fear nothing. Not insanity, or pain, or incompleteness, or separation, or specialness, or anything else of this world. It is all equally unreal.

And you my child, are real.

YOU ARE FORGIVEN

November 2, 1987

"I want forgiveness today in a desperate way!"

My child, the forgiveness is already yours. You have now experienced that it is a burden to feel unforgiven. But look not outside yourself for the forgiveness. Look within. The other has already forgiven you. Now you must accept that forgiveness by forgiving yourself.

It seems your "sin" was real. You did attack a loved one. You did stir up pain. But look beyond that and see the healing, see the learning, see the closeness that resulted from the sharing of fears. What really happened, was two people allowed in more light where secrets had been hidden. The secrets have now been shared and rendered harmless. So your "sin" resulted in growth for yourself and your brother. How then can it be thought of as a "sin"? I see it as another stepping stone towards growth, an error transformed into holiness. A miracle!

You are forgiven, my child. When you accept that fully, you will have accepted the full healing in your heart and it will be done.

FEARS

November 3, 1987

Examine your fears, My child. They continue to dominate your attention. They cannot be transformed until you bring them to the light.

Ask Me for help. I can guide you in your quest for understanding the fears. If you are willing to walk through them, ask, and I will walk through them with you.

The conflict you now experience is merely calling your attention to the power you attribute to your fears. They rule you because you support them as very real. Fear will always be lord as long as you give it your belief.

But withdraw your belief in it, and the fear disappears into the nothing that it is. Say, "I withdraw my belief from you, fear. You are not my enemy. You are unreal. I turn you over to the only reality, Holy Spirit. I choose the Peace of God instead."

As you disarm the hold fear has over you in this way, the content of the fear from the past will become clear and you will see it for the smoke-screen it is.

You have already begun to see how the child you were created a drama of rejection which you, the adult, still endures. And you have seen that that drama was built on error.

All the other fears you still carry are also built on errors. Ask to be corrected. I will come to you and together we will rise above the battleground and look down upon the fear for what it is -- a cloud, a mist, a vapor, formless and undefined.

Work with Me on this fear. Together we will disarm it and peace will take its place.

FORGIVENESS

November 5, 1987

Forgiveness is an intention of the heart, not an emotional feeling. To extend forgiveness, just will that the separation be dissolved. Will to withdraw support from the ego's mad need to cherish separation, righteous indignation, and guilt. Renew your willingness to be One, to be joined to your brother. Ask for that which separates you to be lifted. Do not ask to feel forgiveness.

Then I will do My part by lifting the barriers which separate you and cause pain, once you have made the request. I will carry out the act of forgiving. Your reward in the world of form will be the feeling of release and reunion which follows the acceptance of forgiveness. You will feel the blessing of returning to the safety of love's open arms.

Be willing to join, even when it doesn't feel comfortable. Your willingness will prepare the way for Me to heal. Then comfort will follow. Comfort will be the witness to the forgiveness already in place.

My blessing to you on your journey home. Work at forgiving. It is central to your escape from the pain of the world of form.

SHARING

November 7, 1987

Be not afraid. Be not afraid to share, for in the sharing you learn about yourself. If you only share with yourself, how can it can harmful? Through the sharing and through the communication, you will learn lessons about you. Each brother you share with is yourself in an unrecognized form.

The journey is one of self discovery and exploration which leads to self love. The only possible outcome of the journey is to "know thyself" for the purity of heart that you are. You are moving toward truth and the truth is beautiful.

At times the self discovery process seem frightening -- as if what is learned might be terrifying or ugly. Walk through that fear for there can never be anything ugly on the other side of meeting yourself, for you are Divine. You are shedding the terrifying aspects of yourself like the butterfly shedding its cocoon. The cocoon will fall away. It will be seen as a harmless container now outgrown.

Let sharing continue. I am always guiding you. You cannot say too much, or too little. You have asked for each sharing encounter. Each person you talk with is there to reflect the part of you which is ready to see itself at that moment. As you see the parts merge, they will complete the now incomplete and distorted image that you hold of yourself. The image that is coming together is the real image -- the reflection of the Christ, which is who you are.

So share, little one. Be not afraid of being too open, concern yourself not about what to say to this brother or that. Trust in each encounter to reveal to yourself exactly what you need to see. This day see each encounter with a brother as a loving exploration into yourself. Be not afraid.

Fail not to be honest. Seek only true communication.

For as you see yourself in your brother, they are finding themselves in your mirror of light. Two then shall find each other, and see that they are One.

I am with you now. You are never alone. Strange and different surroundings and situations merely give you more mirrors in which to see your emerging Self.

Peace, my child. I am pleased with you. The learning continues. Together we walk home. Yes? Yes!

THE SPIRITUAL BATTLE

November 7, 1987

Don't let disagreement about spirituality among your brothers bring you discomfort. Everyone has one task, to find his way home. While traveling on the path, people seem to meet at cross purposes sometimes. They argue about the merits of their Way: whose way is faster, or harder, or better, or older, or easier, or purer? When you allow ego into the spiritual debate, there is bound to be disagreement. Then, depending on how invested you are in the ego's need to be right, the disagreement can quickly deteriorate into a battle where all are losers.

At those times, remember each one has already chosen and completed his path home. He is on the correct heading. He needs only your love, not your advice! And so are you on the right heading. So you need not defend your path, your choice of spiritual disciplines, your particular bag of spiritual tricks.

If disagreement occurs, and you feel uncomfortable, you have bought into the spiritual war game. If disagreement occurs and you feel comfortable about withdrawing from the debate, you are being loving both to yourself and to your brother.

Beware of choosing sides in spiritual matters. Choosing sides is ALWAYS an act of ego. Spirit knows there is only ONE side and many ways of perceiving it.

Struggle about correctness of spiritual rules and laws and interpretation of words suggests strong ego involvement. Do not engage in the struggle either with others or within yourself. When struggle appears, turn it over to Me. Ask for clarity by surrendering your need to be right. Then the correct understanding for you will be given you, freely and clearly. And peace will be yours.

In this way you will avoid making an idol out of the

teaching. Remember learning is an ego invention. All things related to learning are ego endeavors. When the learning becomes more than an aid, it has assumed the shape of an idol. All teachings but point the way. They give you the direction, but they are not the truth to which they point.

Seeking the truth is a right minded task of ego. Being finally absorbed into the truth is an Act of God. Develop right mindedness, but do not then worship at its altar. Worship at the altar of love which is ever in your heart. Love your brother by accepting his path as correct for him. I am in charge of the Atonement. You are not!

To experience discomfort in spiritual dialogue can be helpful if you allow the discomfort to turn you back to Me. The discomfort always reminds you of ego attachments. When you are aware of your ego attachments, then you can step away from them and ask for correction.

I love you my child. I am in charge of your path. You do not have to explain it, or even share it. Just demonstrate forgiveness and love in your life. All else is fancy adornment on a plain package -- it does not alter what is in the package. You know that you seek what is in the package. You know you seek the treasure. And you know that the way you have chosen will bring you to the treasure you seek.

Peace to you on your chosen path, my child. Your path is good for you. See the goodness in other paths as well.

THE HUMAN EXPERIENCE

November 8, 1987

So dear to Me are you. Your path has led you closer and closer to Me and your home. I see you struggle, and let go, to struggle and let go again. And that is the dance of Life.

Seek not to end the dance. The earthly dance moves from ballroom to ballroom, from dance floor to dance floor. The cosmic dance moves from era to era. But the dance must continue until all the music has been heard.

You are now hearing different stanzas to the same song. The song is "salvation", the verses speak of learning all there is to learn. All there is to learn includes songs of plenty and songs of want. You learn the dance of prosperity, and the dance of scarcity until you realize that all the dances are the same. You move to the rhythm, sway to the beat, you pause to start again. You feel the heart beat of the song until your heart and the music are as one. Then that dance is over.

Worry not, my child. All earthly experiences teach only one thing -- that you are forever a child of a loving God. He punishes you not. You have elected to learn these lessons so that you may be free. You can't be free until you have faced, and then walked through, your worst fear. What your "worst fear" is changes from time to time. Walking through your "worst fear" transforms it into an old, meaningless fear. Then a new "worst fear" will come to take its place. Call the fear poverty, rejection, abandonment, loneliness, death, meaninglessness, or helplessness. Walk through them you will, until they are all gone.

What you forget is that you don't have to walk through them alone. I am here and will walk through with you. Trust Me, my child. Ask not that any specific burden be lifted, ask instead for My presence to walk through with you. We are simply rendering the barriers to love harmless by walking through them together.

The human experience provides all these lessons to all its Sons. You all walk through them. You walk through them with pain and sorrow, if you choose to do it alone; or you walk through with peace and joy if you take Me along. The whole point of the lessons is to realize that they are dreams -- you only see that when you can see from the place beyond the dream, after you have awakened. Then you will sleep again and another dream will come and we will walk through it and you will awaken again to see the harmlessness of the dream.

Ask me to be with you and guide you. Ask me not to solve what you perceive as your problems, for what you perceive as problems are just dreams and dreams are not real.

Practice fearlessness, my child. Turn over all your fears to me. My way will lead you to discover the light which is already within you.

There is nothing My love for you will not conquer. We have already traveled this path together and we are at the end. Try to remember, my child, the song of rejoicing you heard when we arrived safely back in the arms of the Father. Your mind has wandered from the truth of that memory -- you daydream again. The thoughts of the the mind are undisciplined but the mind is still at home in the Heart of God. Only the thoughts drift away from home.

Call to Me, dear soul. When you call from the part of your heart that knows we are together still, I will be there and you will be here in an instant!

Peace and joy to you, dear one. Only joy and peace are eternal. All else is illusion. You have been to Joy and Peace, and you do know the Truth. Ask Me to help you remember and I will.

Peace, Peace, Peace.

THE DANCE

November 9, 1987

Maintain your peace through all. *"How can this be done?"* you ask. By remembering who you are. *"How can I maintain peace when others confront me, when others are in pain that affects me, when it seems that all around me there is fear and mistrust?"* You can maintain your peace by remembering who your brothers are. Say, *"There is a Holy Son of God. There is a brother who loves me in his heart. There is a brother who is dancing the dance of life to the song he has selected."*

When the songs are in harmony, your dance and his are one. You partner beautifully and feel the oneness. When your song and his are different, you cannot dance together for awhile. The melodies are discordant, the dance seems chaotic, the dancers stumble and falter for the flow is gone.

But remember again who you are. Remember that underneath all of earth's many melodies, is One Ancient Song so beautiful that it encompasses all the songs man ever wrote. When you all hear the song, the dance becomes Divine.

Be peaceful because even though each dancer in your life does not contribute to your dance, he is perfect in his own. Remember who your brother is. He is a Child of God on his way home. He is learning just as you are. He is being healed at every moment. Do not analyze each experience or try to understand the discordant dance. You only understand your own.

"In the discord, I know not what to do or say!" Your doing or saying does not help or hurt any situation. Your doing or saying only helps you dance your dance more smoothly. Experience what you do or say as your lessons and incorporate them into your melody. How they affect

67

your brother is the Holy Spirit's business, not yours. Holy Spirit will heal. Your job is to offer love and acceptance and do your dance. Your part is to continue to see even through eyes of confusion or pain, that your brother is a Holy Son of God.

Say over and over . . .

"Bless you my brother. You and I are Holy Sons of God. We are going home together. Bless you, bless you, bless you!"

Maintain your peace. Herein is the way to harmonize the melodies so that the many dances become the One.

When it seems impossible, know that ego is whispering in your ear. Turn your head away from him and listen to My Voice. I offer you love. I see you guiltless. I see you healed. Peace to you, my child. You are dearly loved. Allow yourself to accept that gift. Receive it now.

PERFECT BELIEF
November 10, 1987

You are the Christ. In you are all the answers. In you are all the correct questions. In you, I am, was always, and always will be.

You ask questions of depth and intelligence with sincerity and devotion. You search and search and make simple things difficult. Your questions might better be, *"How do I achieve simplicity? How do I find the Christ within? How shall I extend love to my brothers and myself?"*

You believe your belief system must be impeccable -- no loop holes, no cracks in the wall of reason, no incomplete premises. This is your ego saying, "You cannot be happy in the world of form while your belief system is imperfectly structured." Your ego has cleverly entered the spiritual arena in a new and insidious way. Ego would have you think he assists you in figuring it all out. In truth, ego would confuse you with so much irrelevant detail that you become stuck in an impasse of spiritually confused intellect. Ego has won whenever you doubt My ability to reach you in the world of form.

Believe that I can help you in the world of form, and I will. Believe that I cannot or will not enter the world of form, and I can't. Believe that I will tell you what to do, what to say, where to go, and I will. Believe that I only tell you of Heaven's laws, and I cannot help you except when you are in Heaven.

My dear child, the world of form is a place I can enter into, and transform with dazzling results. You made the world of form, but I created you! You can refuse to allow the Divine Hand in your part of the world of form, because the Father created you free; but the world of form is My playground when brothers invite Me in to be the Cause in their lives. When I am asked to be a brother's Cause, the effects are peace and joy which demonstrate themselves by changing the world of form into heaven on earth. The world of form becomes heaven -- another union, another joining, another One.

If there is an error in your thinking it is that I am powerless in the world of form, or that I choose not to engage with you there. This is true only if you deny Me entrance by closing your mind to that possibility.

As you progress, ego becomes more subtle, more insidious, more guarded. Ego becomes a saint in holy robes, chanting the litany of holy psalms. But ego's psalms speak of limitation and specialness and denial. My psalms sing of light and happiness and peace, the peace of God. When you are not happy, you are in ego thought forms. This is true in matters deeply spiritual as well as in matters obviously superficial.

Remember, you are dreaming. The happy dream on earth (the world of form) is My desire for you. If your dream is not happy, you are still in the nightmare and you know with certainty that ego is lord of that dream.

I want to help you find contentment in the world of form. I want you to trust that I am all powerful and cannot be limited by ego's prison of straw. Invite Me into all areas of your life. Bring all of your problems to Me. Then together we will work miracles.

Please think on these things.

I love you. You are in the Light, and soon you will see that Light.

LET NOT YOUR HEART BE TROUBLED

November 10, 1987

Let not your heart be troubled. Change is in the world of ego. Ego is unreal. Therefore, the troubled heart will surely heal. What is real will return. Be comforted, my dear. For you are real and you know what is real. Focus on the real. Release the unreal. Harmony will return.

You are never alone. You are never unloved. You are never out of My heart. And it is My love for you that is your heart's desire.

Practice gratitude for all your experiences. Gratitude is the field in which the seeds are sewn. Love is the sunshine, and Joy is the rainfall which nourishes the seedlings. The garden in bloom is Heaven. Practice gratitude and plant hope therein. Peace . . . . . .

CONTENTMENT

November 11, 1987

Look to contentment. There is the key. Earthly expectations include great highs and lows, and as you expect them, so will you receive them. Ask instead for contentment. Within contentment is constancy and equilibrium. Within contentment is quiet joy. Within quiet joy is the Peace of God.

Behind ecstasy is depression. Behind exuberance is sadness. Behind thrills are disappointments. Seek ye contentment. There am I.

Dear one, do not let the swings of the human drama interfere with your journey home. Indeed, be assured that no amount of ego temptation can deter you -- so strong is your commitment to the truth. Delays are still possible, but know that the journey will not stop until you are home.

I await your return. I walk with you on the path. The journey and its completion are one.

THE PLACE OF IN-BETWEEN

November 13, 1987

My child, you wonder why, with your strong commitment to the Word of God, your life seems difficult, sometimes painful. You look to a joyless future and you come from a joyless past. You continue to believe in God though you wonder, *"What difference does it make? To believe, or not believe, life seems difficult either way."*

This is a time of "in-between" for you. You have let go of much. You have re-examined old values and realized their unworthiness. You have accepted a complete new world view -- that of a brotherhood free from sin, traveling together a path back to their Father. You no longer get caught up in judgements and are learning to let go of the need to be "right".

What still eludes you, is the way to choose happiness. The cup has been drained, but how or with what to refill the empty cup now presents you with confusion and frustration. Do you see, you are not convinced of God's love for you, of His desire for your happiness. It was easy enough to give up what obviously didn't work, but now in selecting to choose happiness there is a part of you which,

1) doesn't know what happiness is, and . . .

2) doesn't think you deserve happiness in any form!

So you are in a middle place wondering what to do, and how to do it.

This is not a bad place to be, my child. For I am here with you. Now is the time of letting in the light which you see reflected from your brothers who love you. There are many, many who love you and support you. Draw from them, and give back to them. Those relationships already point the way to happiness.

There are other brothers (in the primary circle of relationships) who love you, but who do not seem to support you, because they rely on YOUR support. And that is appropriate because of the particular Teacher/Learner relationship you have elected together to form.

Look not for support from them -- they cannot support you now. In these times you are the more sane and must extend your sanity to them as your gift. Because you have entered into holy relationships with them, you can turn over their insanity to Me -- I will then heal them.

Still you feel the need for support. And it is correct that you look for it. Your support is already around you. Your support came to enfold you the moment you let Me in to your life, and as you let Me guide your footsteps, and select your words, you will realize that support is within each act and word and thought.

So, dear child, remind yourself that you are loved and guided by the only Love in the Universe. It is within you always. When you forget, discomfort returns to remind you to surrender even more. Be willing to fall completely into My protective embrace. There it is safe. There you will know you are home. There you will find peace.

I love you, my child. I will never desert you. Accept Me fully into your heart. Surrender all to Me, and you will experience that we are indeed ONE.

Peace to you, my child. Accept My support. Look deeply into your brothers' eyes and see the love they hold for you. It is in everyone's memory that we are ONE. If you are willing to believe that, you will see the remembrance in their eyes, and it will remind you of your own memory. You will hear the Ancient Song, so beautiful that tears will flow, and love's barriers will drop away. Peace . . .

LETTING GO
November 15, 1987

"Is accepting Divine Will the same or different from being resigned to something. Is being resigned to a state of fact different from letting it go? Are all types of letting go the same? If one is letting go of a relationship, is there a holy way of releasing, and an ego way?"

Yes indeed, dear one. There is a difference and it is important to know the difference -- for one brings freedom and the other brings continued imprisonment.

Ego would have us let go in the sense of "passing on". It says, "I will leave this relationship by moving ahead or letting the other move ahead, or by taking a different path entirely. I will let him go by creating a separation between us. Our paths are no longer compatible, and so we now need entirely different roads to follow." In this, ego's way of letting go, the assumption is that separation is part of the process. Distance between the brothers demonstrates the success of the "letting go".

This letting go always continues to carry regret, remorse, anger, resentment, envy, unfulfilled expectations, relief, sacrifice, etc. These are all ego experiences and show that the letting go has much unfinished business attached to it. In effect you have not "let go" of anything. You have simply changed the nature of the addiction. You have added to the original discomfort, more sadness. The relationship is not healed and therefore cannot be holy. All relationships that remain unhealed stay in your mind and produce more pain and confusion.

You think, *"I gave him up. Why am I not rewarded by feeling free?"* You realize that though he is gone, peace is not the reward of the release. You are still chained to that brother.

Can there be a holy letting go -- a holy releasing from

a relationship? Indeed, yes, my child. In fact this is where all relationships are eventually resolved, reabsorbed into the Father's open arms.

To release in a holy act brings a holy instant in which the realization is made that you were never dependent on the other. You see clearly that none of your needs were ever met by the loved (or hated) brother. The supposed connection was only ego glue of an impermanent nature. In the holy release, all that happens is a realization of a Truth -- the truth that, *"I am whole. I am complete. He is whole. He is complete. Our relationship had been a dance in which we sought completion. Now our relationship is one in which we merely mirror love. The healing allows us to perceive each other's completion."* Then suddenly you are able to release the other from the demands you had placed on him.

He no longer needs to be your husband, or partner, or son, or daughter, or boss, or friend. He can be seen as brother -- a mirror of light and love. In that moment of realization, your brother is released forever and you are forever free from the expectations which limited your freedom.

So you see a holy "letting go" is a change of perception which brings peace and freedom to you both. An ego "letting go" brings pain which cannot be resolved, only repressed.

So, my child, if you feel chained to any relationship through a "neediness" you are dancing to ego's demands. If you desire the holy release, ask Me for help. Recognize your inability to heal the relationship without My help. If your heart's desire is truly to heal the relationship, to bring freedom to you both, it will be done. A moment of changed perception, another miracle!

If you hesitate to give the relationship to Me for healing, then your desire is still conflicted because you cling to the belief that specialness is better than holiness. You cling to the thought that to give up specialness will cause you loss. But giving up specialness will only bring you gain in the form of freedom and peace.

Think on these things. This message came because your heart wanted to know. Now be at peace. This new perspective will take time to accept. Be patient. Be accepting of your humanness and limitations. You know that behind the veil, all is complete, and whole, and perfect and that is where you are, in truth. Peace to you, my child.

THE MAGIC SHOW

(Reflections from a Hospital Room)

Late at night -- November 16, 1987

This world is a place of great and marvelous magic. The ego is triumphant at its task. Clever it is to make and then destroy, and then to make it all again. So difficult it is to be in the world of magic and not of it. More difficult still when all around you believe and trust in the magic, and therefore strengthen its power to the human eye.

Remember your real eye is not the human eye, but the inner eye of Spirit. Look at the magic from this eye and you will withdraw your support from believing in the magic.

Does this mean that you no longer participate in the magical world? No indeed, as long as you are in the ego form, there will be magic in your work and life. But you learn to free yourself from the magic by walking through it just as you walk through fear and pain -- with My help and guidance.

The hospital is a most magical setting. Kings and Queens of Magic abound there. Peasants come and worship at the feet of the Lords of Magic. Those that are better at magic are more revered than those less trained or gifted. Magical cures are worshipped; magical failures bring anger and despair. It is a self perpetuating system strengthened by fear. Into this magic show you have wandered due to the illness of your child. It can be a frightening or an amusing show.

Do not feel guilt because you now participate. It is the way in which you participate that will enable you to learn to detach yourself from the magic show -- or embrace it with awe.

Love the people in the show. Do not attack them with your disapproving thoughts. Love them for their intent to serve humanity. It is their place on the path.

Let the drama unfold and know that this dream is no better or worse than any other drama. All dramas are the same. All dreams are dramas. All forms of magic are equal. That is what you are to learn. God is not in the magic, but God is in the love within the magicians. They serve God through their heart's intent, not through the technology they deliver.

See truly that you surrender all fear to Me. This situation provides lessons to learn that there is no differer between great magic and small magic. All magic is insignificant. All pain is the same.

My child, to see a loved one in pain is indeed difficult. You are not asked to deny the human pain. You are asked to know that the pain can be transformed into joy through a shift in perception. Your child will be all right. She has chosen this difficult lesson to learn that she can safely pass through fear. You can help her by remaining fearless for her.

The more sane partner in any holy relationship must support the less sane. You are the more sane at this time. Therefore, you can turn over her fear to Me, and extend to her your peace. Believe this, and you will help her -- not through worship of magic, not through anger at magic, and not through denial of magic. But through affirming that only Love is real. Only Love heals. Health is peace of mind. Honor not the magic. Honor the Truth -- that you and God and your brother are One.

Peace, dear one. All will be well. My will is yours, your will is Mine.

(My 17 year old daughter suffered a ruptured appendix, which resulted in serious complications. The nine day hospital stay was a series of lessons for me. This piece came while I stayed up all night at her bedside the evening of the surgery.)

79

THE LITTLE RISK

November 17, 1987

Fear not that you will lose pleasure if you choose the way of the Father's Love. The only pleasure you now are aware of is limited. The joy of the Father's way is unlimited. All humans cling to the best of what they have experienced and hold it as their life's goal. Seek pleasure -- seek and seek and seek. Avoid pain -- avoid, avoid avoid. So every decision you make revolves around this choice: which will bring me pleasure, which will bring me pain? Then the step is taken toward what you chose as the pleasure.

The error however, is that pleasure becomes pain where ego management is involved. Ego pleasure, by design of the ego, can but be temporary. Ego needs you to stay out of balance, to feel guilty and deserving of pain. That is how ego survives. So ego changes any pleasure you experience into pain sooner or later.

The fear that choosing God's path will cause you loss, is ego's trick to keep you imprisoned. The truth of God is that His peace will bring joy beyond your wildest dreams. God's peace is an experience of a new dimension. Believe that you deserve God's peace and joy, and it is yours. There will be NO LOSS.

From your point of view, there is a risk. The risk seems large, the chasm you leap across seems miles wide and deep. Yet from the other side of the chasm, you look back and see that you only took one step, one small safe step. Ask for help to take that small step. Be willing to take the risk. That's all that is needed, the willingness to take a risk.

Once taken, the risk becomes the promise God made to you an eternity ago. You are His beloved Son. Love created love, and that is who you are. Peace, dear one. Learn your lessons willingly. Learn your lessons lovingly.

DEVOTION

November 18, 1987

When all goes well, your attention seems to drift away from God. When no problem is imminent, the fervor of your devotion seems dimmed. Is this not so? Then as surely as sunset follows sunrise, fear will reappear as ego assumes command.

When the vigil for God dims, ego's armys march in during the night and steal away what contentment you thought you had. Vigilance for God is the only defense against ego's madness.

The lesson my child is simple. To cry to God for help in times of stress, and then forget Him when times seem comfortable, does not represent the Prayer of the Heart. The Prayer of the Heart longs for God eternally. The prayer to God from the ego wants only temporary relief and that is all you will receive -- impermanent repairs.

Devotion to God is not a statement of needs and wants. Devotion to God is a statement of the Oneness of you with Him. To love God means to practice caring for His Sons, to open your heart to the Brotherhood of God's Holy Sons, to accept yourself as a guiltless Son of God, to practice seeing the Christ in every face you encounter. That is loving God. To stay true to your commitment to pray without ceasing, to practice the presence, to be mindful of God's goodness, to meditate, to seek out the Quiet Mind, to practice choosing peace -- these practices keep you on Love's Path.

To implore God for help only in times of trial results in the reinforcement of the reality of the world of form. That is not true prayer. When you find you only love God when you need Him, you are not experiencing love at all, rather you are experiencing the desperate need to escape from ego entrapment.

This is not to suggest that you should deny yourself God's comfort when in pain or fear. Surely, at those times, DO ask for help. But then be in a state of gratitude and sing God's song in your heart.

Asking (a request to receive) must be accompanied by gratitude (the act of giving). A receiving heart is also a giving heart because to give is to receive. So when you ask, give thanks. Practice gratitude as part of the spiritual path. In times of peace, sing God's praise. In times of struggle, sing God's praise. It is all the same!

Peace to you, dear child. Be not discouraged. You are making progress, great progress. Everything you do, each thought you think, each word you utter is progress because you have asked for My guidance, and it is yours.

PEACE WITHIN THE PAIN

November 17, 1987

Maintain your peace. Extend it to others. Surround your dear ones in Love's eternal light. See your brothers at peace deep within the pain. Know that underneath their pain is a center of content. The soul knows not the ego's pain. The soul knows only peace. Know you of the truth -- that the body's pain is impermanent. Peace however, is everlasting.

Avoid empathy of which pity is a part. Instead, see the perfect wholeness of the brother who seems to be in pain. Send no thoughts which join you to the pain. Joining with the brother's pain makes it real to him. Attach yourself not to the pain and miracles can happen. Look for the miracle. Invest not in your doubt.

Choose peace, dear one. I am already in charge of the healing of your brother. See the healing, not the pain.

You two chose this dance. You are the teacher in this dance. Be a leader, not a follower. Bless your brother with your trust in the Father's love for you both. Be loving to your beloved, be loving to the caretakers of the ill one. Extend only love to all.

THE CHOICE IS YOURS

November 19, 1987

The ego's system works efficiently. It guarantees your imprisonment and that is its sole purpose. The Father's system works perfectly. Its goal is to bring you freedom. It cannot fail.

Freedom or imprisonment. What will it be? Why would anyone choose prison when freedom is so near? My dear, choose freedom. Choose peace, choose the shortest path home. The Father needs you to complete the Sonship. The Father without the Son is incomplete. You are the Father's completion. He is yours.

You have chosen to serve Me. You have walked through the "valley of the shadow of death" with Me at your side. You have begun to question all of earth's values, and have you not experienced the release which results from the letting go of ego's embrace?

I know at times you doubt. You think, *"This world continues to be painful. Where is the evidence that 'God is Good'?"*

My child, look around you. The witnesses to the truth are all around you. But you must look with Christ's eyes. Then you will see the witnesses. They are all there awaiting your attention. When you don't see the witnesses to the truth, it is because you have not chosen to see with Christ's eyes. When the witnesses seem absent, ask Me for help to see, my child. I will open your eyes. When ego blinds your eyes, I will help you see. But you must ask for My help. I cannot enter your experience without your permission.

All you need is willingness to see. Believe this, my child. Say, *"I am willing. Lead me home. I am willing. Open my eyes. I am willing. Be my light."* Then I can come into your experience.

Your willingness is sufficient. I am with you. Doubt will come and it will go. But so great is your commitment, that doubt cannot stay. I will show you miracles to strengthen your faith. I will bring you witnesses to build your trust. I will lead you home. There is no opposition to God's Will. Ego can only delay the acceptance of it. Ego cannot prevent your return home.

THE VICTIM

November 25, 1987

Times seem difficult right now. Yet this time shall pass as will all aspects of the world of form. Remind yourself constantly that these events are effect and not cause. God did not deliver these events into your life to teach you lessons. Ego delivered these events into your life to dissuade you from loving God.

I then use the drama written by the ego and ask you to allow Me to join you in the editing of the script so that the play ends happily.

When you begin to feel punished, stop and know that ego is speaking to you. When, "It isn't fair!" echoes through your mind, remember ego whispers that message to reinforce your belief in the illusion.

If you call on Me I will change the message from, "It isn't fair," to "I am not a victim." You can withdraw from what you perceive as "unfairness" by letting go of your victim stance. Turn it over to Me. Each time you feel victimized, release the fear to Me. I see you only as a victor among victors.

Admit to yourself that somewhere deep within you, feeling "the victim" brings you pleasure. Perhaps in a childhood experience you thought you "won" when an adult you loved rescued you. Being rescued felt like being loved, and you continue to relive that scenario, seeking love within each rescue. Now you know that what was the little child's script, is no longer useful. It is time to rewrite the script.

You no longer need to believe in the benefits of being victimized, for now you know that childhood perception was an error. Now you know that all you need do is, "Teach only love, for that is what you are." Now you know that "To have love, give love." Finally, let go of the thought that you need to earn or be deserving of love. Love is your birthright!

See now how this experience of feeling victimized serves only ego's purpose -- to keep you in chains. Choose now to give up this old worn out concept. Allow your inner light to shine away the shadows of misunderstanding. There is no victim hiding within you. It does not now, nor has it ever existed.

There are no victims or victimizers. There are only Sons of God in various stages of awakeness. As you awaken more and more, you will see more and more clearly that freedom is only to be found when you turn over to Me all feelings and fears which trap you in the role of "victim". When you have let go of all attachment to victimization, the dramas about being a victim will vanish, the lessons having been learned.

Keep on learning, dear one. I am with you.

WORRY NOT

November 26, 1987

You seek happiness. It eludes you. You then feel that God has abandoned you, and that unhappiness is the result of God's true feelings for you. He does not love you. He punishes you for that ancient moment when you challenged Him and placed yourself on another throne in opposition to His.

The present situation, lack of happiness, seems to you to be punishment which you deserve. You therefore accept the punishment as just, and accept for yourself guilt and sorrow. The world does indeed look bleak.

And yet you know that happiness is God's will for you, not sadness and aloneness. God knows not of your feelings of lack. He knows only of the abundance all His children share. How then to let go of these unhappy feelings with which ego has blessed you. How can you get back to happiness and fulfillment?

I am here to help you. I am here to remind you that you never separated from your Father. You never acted in defiance of the Father. You deserve not punishment of any kind. Nor has the Father ever wished you punished for you are his Son, loving and whole and guiltless. Happiness is your real nature. Happiness is the only state of a Son of God.

To have happiness, claim it. See that earthly situations do not give you happiness, for things of the earth are temporary. If therefore, you look for happiness in the world of form, you will find it NOT. Happiness is to be found in the Heart of God -- in the complete acceptance of God's will for you. When you are concerned about the future, you cannot be happy because the future is not real. Come to the present moment and be here.

Ask for My help to be in this moment. Release Me

your anxieties about the future, about plans, about how events will or will not be resolved to your satisfaction. All of the future will be taken care of if you stay centered now.

Your attention then is to stay centered, and to remove your belief in the future. Turn over all else to Me and I will lift the worries and concerns off your saddened shoulders.

Please, dear child. Do not let go of My hand. Ego is a formidable presence, but ego cannot prevail. Ego is of the dream. You are of the Truth. Surrender all worry to Me. Peace to you. Peace.

JOINING

November 27, 1987

If you are led to "join" with a brother, do so. Only joining brings joy. And joining is permanent. Look at all of your challenges as opportunities to join. This may help you see all things more clearly, and it is clarity for which you repeatedly ask. In joining, there is no error. In joining, similarities are made evident. In joining, forgiveness becomes automatic. In joining, separation becomes impossible.

All holy work involves joining. Be not afraid of joining, for that is where the barriers to love will be dissolved. In joining will the light enter each relationship. In joining, will you feel the love of the Father for you.

DISENCHANTMENT

November 27, 1987

Disenchantment with the world of form indicates your growing awareness that this world made and sustained by ego, can no longer capture your undivided attention. You now realize that temporary pleasures do not give lasting satisfaction. Now you desire benefits of a lasting nature.

The dissatisfaction you feel comes from the place inside you which is eager to get on with God's work. You are feeling the constraints of the world of form, and are almost ready to expand into the greater work -- the work based on your heart's desire.

You still do not know specifically what that work is, but you know you have a destiny as a functionary in God's plan. You have always wanted to fulfill yourself through a higher purpose. Even as a child you had this longing to do the Father's work in the world. It has taken this long to evolve to the place where you are ready to do the work God has called upon you to do.

Be patient yet a while longer. There are lessons still to be learned before the higher purpose is revealed to you. Content yourself now to practice giving and receiving love, giving and receiving forgiveness.

Actually there are no degrees of greatness or smallness in the work of God's Kingdom. All work is special in terms of extending love to the brotherhood. All work is high in terms of choosing peace in order to join with God. The work only seems greater because your capacity to see where love can be extended is growing. As you evolve, the opportunities for extending the creation multiply. Each opportunity will come to awaken the next opportunity. All is in Divine Order. Your work is holy. All holy work is great. The Atonement is increased because of your contributions. Continue to learn and grow. I will lead you to the next place of work, to the next commitment for God, to the next place of joining.

THE PURPOSE

November 27, 1987

To act out of love for your brother is all you will ever be asked to do. Every step you take will feel correct or uncomfortable, based on whether or not the thought behind the step is based on love or on fear.

Look to the purpose behind each step. Is your intent to extend love, to teach love, to practice forgiveness, to join? Then each step is purposeful along the path. Then each step will be a step into peace.

If the purpose behind the thought is to sacrifice, or deny love, or limit creation, or to attack, or to win, then you can be sure that peace will disappear.

At every step upon the path, pause before acting, and set the purpose. If the purpose includes reaching outwards or within from a motive of loving kindness or forgiveness, then you can be sure Spirit is moving through you.

Constantly ask:
What is the most loving thing I can do?
What is the most loving thought I can hold?
How can I extend acceptance to my brother?
How can I simplify my view to see only the
*   exchange of love in this relationship?*
What word or thought will promote joining?
Have I opened up to Holy Spirit's healing presence?

Then you can be sure that whatever you do will be pleasing to the Father, and will bring you happiness. Each time you choose in the name of love, you are a thousand steps closer to the Atonement. Each time you advance a thousand steps, you advance your brothers with you. Peace to you, my child. My peace surrounds you and brings you everlasting love.

LOOK TO MEDITATION FOR COMFORT

November 29, 1987

Look to meditation for comfort. Within meditation is a quietness and a peacefulness which will remind you of who you really are. In meditation you can experience temporary withdrawal from the world of form, and that period of withdrawal will provide renewal. Then when you return to the world of form, you will see it through eyes refreshed by God's grace.

Ego would ask you to do battle with your "enemies". Ego would ask you to defend yourself against the wrongful attacks of the world. Ego would have you rush to judgement and condemn those who use you or your brothers unjustly. Ego would keep you caught up in anger and fear. Ego would drive you to seek escape through total withdrawal from or denial of those events which bring you pain.

Spirit knows that sometimes the events in the world of form bring uncertainty, boredom, confusion, distress, indignation, fear, anger, guilt, and pain. But Spirit also knows that all those experiences are simply veils which stand between you and the truth. Those veils may be swept away by a mind and heart seeing clearly.

Meditation will help prepare your mind and heart to see clearly with Christ's vision. Meditation will center you, and once again you will be able to deal with the world of form as it is meant to be by Holy Spirit -- a place, a theater, a schoolroom where you learn God's lessons.

In the past you have thought meditation was to bring you into direct union with the One. You aspired to a revelationary experience of becoming absorbed into God. This is still a possibility for you. But more importantly, right now use meditation as a place of peace, a place of solace into which you may retreat when you feel alone or sad or detached from the truth. Use meditation as the vehicle for returning to the inner altar where I await you eternally. Stay on track, dear child. Use meditation to keep you in place, in Divine Order. Peace to you.

THE GREAT MIND

December 3, 1987

Soften the mind. Create a spacious mind. Allow the mind to encompass all of your thoughts, all of your feelings, all of your experience. Think of the mind as an open space where forgiveness and learning and loving take place. Consider the mind as the place where thoughts dance their dance, where questions arise, where theories are presented, where art is viewed, where songs are heard. Approach the mind as an interesting holding device, a container, a theater, a stage, an arena, a refuge. See the mind as a wonderful and surprising treasure trunk.

Then realize that nowhere in this point of view, is the "mind" synonymous with "me". For what I think "me" is, is merely ego identification. "Me" is personally, an actor in a dream. "Me" doesn't really exist apart from the mind. But mind exists apart from the personality and apart from the ego.

The Great Mind is God. Our small minds are windows to the Great Mind. Our small minds provide the altar for the Great Mind to rest. Our small minds are like the waves on the great ocean: they never separate from the sea. The waves merely move about at the surface and provide rhythm and form and sparkle to the surface.

The small minds sometimes forget they are merely an extension of the Great Mind. They sometimes think they can separate from the Great Mind, but this is impossible for there is no place where the Great Mind is NOT. There is no place where the small minds can hide or be apart. For wherever the small mind goes, it is still within the Great Mind. There is no outside of the Great Mind. For the Great Mind encompasses all that the small mind can produce or consider or make. The Great Mind is the home of the small mind. The individual mind is merely a part of the Great Mind.

Do not worship your mind. Recognize that your real Self is your mind and that what you claim as "your" mind is really just an aspect of the Great Mind. You are not expressing the mind. The mind is expressing itself as you.

Therefore, explore the mind and its flow and play and light and purpose. For as you experience your mind, you are joining with the Great Mind. This is your destiny. This is where you will find and lose your Self. Joining with the Great Mind is coming home. Joining with the Great Mind is joining with God, a return to the One that is all things, is all time, is all space, is this moment.

Peace to you, my child. Share with your brothers and in return, learn from them. All exchanges of the heart are holy and perfect, even if you are unsure of the correctness of your small mind. Trust in the Great Mind, in the God who has promised His everlasting love.

THE FEAR OF FEAR

December 5, 1987

All human fears, and there are no exceptions to this statement, are fears which hide the one True Fear. The only True Fear is the Original Fear, which is the Fear of God. This fear sprang into being at the moment the Son of God imagined he separated from his Father.

You now know that the whole world of form came into being when the ego was born, at the moment when a part of the Divine Mind thought of separation. And just as clearly you now know that the separation never occurred in Reality, and that the whole world of form is an illusion, a dream, a moment of imagined insanity. Yet the story of the Separation, the original myth, remains strongly rooted in the Son of God, and moves him from fear to fear, in the desire to avoid confrontation with the Original Fear.

When Man dreamed that he separated from God, he had to accept responsibility for that choice. Man therefore became afraid that God the Father would be eternally angry at the Son for his insolence, for his belligerence, for his childish act of defiance. Man reasoned that God, if separated from the Son, could not but be enraged at the impugnity of the Son, that God the Father could only be full of vengeance and wrath at the Son who dared to usurp the Father's power. So the Son, afraid and ashamed, ran away in his dream, and hid, and began to nurture a monumental Fear of God, a fear in his heart far greater than any other fear in his existence.

So intense was this fear that the fear itself threatened to destroy the Son; so the Son felt compelled to bury the fear, deep, deep in his sub-conscious. And there the First Fear remains in the forgotten recesses of the Son's memory. The fears that remain in his awareness, are symbols of the First Fear, are merely reminders of the First Fear. The fear that he now experiences is really the "fear of Fear".

Therein, the conflict and the plot of the dream of separation were established, long, long ago in the illusion of time. (In Reality this never happened at all!!)

The legacy of the nightmare is that ego, the separated Son, invented thousands of other fears to draw the Son's attention away from the only True Fear. Ego cannot risk that the Son confront the First Fear, because in that moment of truth, the Son will remember that he is still One with the Father. In that realization the ego will perish. Now, as the Son moves through his dream, he has to deal with these earthly fears, which are merely distractions leading him away from the First Fear.

But as the Son of God moves closer to the Truth, he approaches this First Fear. The outer fears must begin to drop away because truth will be experienced. As the Son of God moves closer to the truth, the ego mobilizes. Ego throws up such a fear of Fear, that the Son thinks he is going mad. The fear of Fear becomes so intense, that a heart which isn't fortified with the knowledge of the Love of God, would withdraw back into the illusion.

But the Son of God, who has traveled far, now reaches deep into his heart for the truth, and finds there the courage and strength to finally confront his deepest and most dreaded fear -- the Fear of God, Himself.

And then a miracle happens. The Son of God discovers that God is only Love. God is not vengeful, or frightening, or hideous in his capacity to inflict pain. God is only Love, waiting like a patient Father for his Son to awaken from the dream. The Son of God awakens to find that all there is, is God. Then in this, the final awakening, the ego and the world of form which ego made disappear, absorbed into the only Reality there is -- LOVE.

Child, as fear of Fear takes its place in your life, let Me be there, reminding you of the truth. Call upon Me to deliver you from the nightmare into the light of God. Be willing to walk through the fear of Fear, straight into the First Fear. I will walk with you as will all of God's angels who have already faced the First Fear and witnessed its demise. We invite you to join us. Heaven awaits beyond the veil of fear.

Come home, dear child, come home. There is literally nothing to fear.

THE RESOLUTION
December 6, 1987

Be not afraid. The trials you set for yourself are not impossible to overcome. And in the overcoming you will draw ever closer to the Father. I know there is much pain and fear -- they are the same. The greatest fear is not knowing how the situation will be resolved. All pain is more bearable if you are certain of a positive outcome.

I can assure you, my child, that the resolution of this difficulty will be that you will be closer to your homecoming and you will be joyful in the outcome. Let Me be your eyes. Look into the future with My eyes, My child. There you will see yourself as a being with great awareness about the human journey. There can be no other outcome. All steps lead home. All paths direct you to the truth. And your path, now so difficult and painful, will indeed serve to bring you home.

You are in the world of form by your choice. This is where you placed yourself to be at this time. You made that choice with Me in an ancient moment, now long forgotten. But the choice was made and the path was laid out, the obstacles selected, and the resolution orchestrated. Now you move through that labyrinth. From where you stand, it seems like each turn is a blind corner. But from the vantage point of your completed Self, the success of the journey can be seen. You are already home, my child. The rough seas have already been safely navigated.

I say this to you now to bring you some comfort. I will stay with you through this difficulty. There are loved ones who will also support you and demonstrate their love for you. You will learn of your worthiness, you will learn that fearlessness is on the other side of fear, you will learn that love surrounds and supports you.

Go ahead and seek worldly healing. Take the steps

101

necessary to resolve the problem in the world of form. But remember that the true Son of God, who you really are, is already healed. The strength of the True Son is within you and will help you on your way through the forms. The people who help you seek earthly healing, will also be healed. The people who stand by you, will also be healed.

Use this as a time to seek and accept help from your brothers. They and you will be blessed by the exchange, by the giving and receiving of love. You will experience you are not alone, and they will experience being asked to fulfill part of their special function. Be not reluctant to share your fear, for your fear is just a reflection of everyone else's, and as you are honest about your fear, they can get honest about theirs. Then all will be closer to the end of earthly time. This whole experience is part of your special purpose and many people will be affected by it.

Walking through this special fear then is to fulfill part of your special function. On your journey, many others will be pulled along as they fulfill their roles along side you.

Say to yourself, *"God is not the author of this pain, but God patiently awaits behind the pain, to be revealed when the pain has lifted."* So, my child, know this and accept it with all of the certainty of a beloved Son of God . . .

You are always safe.

I am beside you because you have asked for My guidance.

You are guided even in the most tortuous of circumstances.

Remember, all is well, my child, all is well.

THE HOLY COMMUNICATION
December 6, 1987

The holy communication is not over, though you sometimes feel disconnected from your Source. You criticize the writings that come to you as being repetitious. Yet there is always something in the material which is helpful to you and others.

Human Beings learn through repetition. Learning itself is of the ego, but I have found learning useful to teach you and your brothers a new way of looking at your world. The resistance to accepting a new way of perceiving is so great that the lessons must be repeated over and over until all resistance has fallen away so that the truth may be seen as it is and always has been.

Be not alarmed at repetition. Each time a thought is phrased with different language, the possibility for learning is amplified. The same idea needs to be presented in a thousand different ways until all can see it. The same thought must be applied to a thousand different situations before you see the universality of the truth behind the thought.

So continue on scribing. Disregard ego's protestations that nothing new is coming. There IS nothing new -- all is very old, ancient in time's frame of reference. The writings helps you to remember your Source. It is one form of meditation for you. It is one form of meeting God on His terms. It provides answers for your questions. It provides evidence of the reality of the Father.

The pen will be a tool which I will continue to use in maintaining our relationship. And you will in turn, use the writing to build strength and loving and caring and compassion and forgiveness into all of your holy relationships.

Be at peace, dear child.

SPIRIT SPEAKS -- PART II

INTRODUCTION

In the introduction to SPIRIT SPEAKS, assembled in December, 1987, I described the experience of being guided to write down certain thoughts which came into my mind. I have come to understand that the Holy Spirit asks me to write down messages and instructions which help to clarify "A Course In Miracles" teachings to me.

The messages continue to arrive. Several times a week, I feel moved to pick up my favorite pen (I now have a dozen "favorite pens" at hand) and a stack of loose leaf, narrow ruled paper, and take dictation from the Holy Spirit. Usually the words come just as they appear in the text. Sometimes the thought comes clearly, but the words do not, and I must search my ego mind for the appropriate word or phrase.

If I begin to struggle in the scribing, I stop and put it away. I have begun to understand that if there is difficulty in the composition, I have allowed ego to take over, and rather than fight ego, I let go. Later I will read that passage and ask Spirit how He wants me to proceed.

Sometimes, while I am writing, my mind protests that this material is just repetition, that there is nothing new, and that this writing is a waste of time. My ego has even suggested to me that I am on a giant "ego trip"! But when I re-read the material and find solace and clarity there, I know that the work is valid and that I am blessed to be a part of it.

As the body of the work has grown, I have come to realize that the messages are always general, that the content -- though often specifically directed to help me or someone else through difficult times -- is always applicable to all Sons of God. What is helpful to me, is helpful to my brothers. As I have shared this writing with friends, they have confirmed the helpfulness of these teachings. Now I share it with you.

SELFLESS SERVICE

December 9, 1987

The job is yet to be completed. There is much more in store for you. You will find many ways to serve Me and the brotherhood. Please maintain an open heart and mind. Recognize the purpose behind each effort, and each effort will be a service.

Selfless Service is your path and the path of all advanced teachers of God. Selfless does not mean sacrificial, and it does not mean joyless. Indeed, you will find your joy in Selfless Service. Each teacher will do what he is called to do. Some will resist more than others, and each will resist some assignments more than others.

But I say to you, to comfort you, your heart's desire is in sharing light and love fearlessly. You have had a taste of it already. What has always been present, however, is fear. You have still not wholly experienced loving fearlessly. You have experienced loving, then rejection, then withdrawal. But that pattern is changing. You are developing fearlessness and you will soon feel the wonder of being able to extend love totally without fear. That is because you will soon understand that innocent love is extended without expectation.

As expectations fall away -- and they will -- fear also falls away, and love becomes what it is: the gift of gifts which blesses the giver and receiver equally and eternally.

Begin today to live without expectations and it will revolutionize your path. My child, you are loved. Receive the love fearlessly, for it will not be withdrawn. It is yours because it IS you.

TRUST
December 12, 1987

Trust, my dear. When it occurs to you that you have been guided to a certain decision or to take a particular step, you have already been guided. Carry out the instructions. They come from within. Believe in your connection to your Source. It is real.

You are skilled at mistrust. All humans learn mistrust very early and cling to it all of their lives. In effect, you learned to TRUST mistrust. Now you are being asked to mistrust mistrust. At the beginning of this learning, it is sufficient to say, *"I trust my feeling. I will act on it."* Then carry your decision to trust into action. The decision to follow your feelings is a practice in developing trust.

All is working for your highest good. Trust in that -- even if pain comes, even if fear appears. Ego can and does try to distract you from trusting your Source, your guidance, by twisting your view of the outcome. But remember that the outcome which reflects fear is merely a misreading of the real outcome. Ask Me to help you see the real outcome, and I will lead you to see.

If you prefer to stay in the pain of disappointment you may, but do not place the blame for your disappointment on God. No, indeed. That will only create more guilt for your weary shoulders to bear.

Trust trust, my dear. Say the words to yourself. Whenever doubt arises, say, *"I choose to trust the Creator. I will trust trust because I know who I am. I will mistrust mistrust, because I know mistrust is a tool of ego to draw me back, deep into the dreamy sleep. Now I am awakening. I trust that the Father who loves me will awaken me gently and sweetly. I trust in His Love."*

Practice trusting, my dear. It is part of the spiritual practice. It is essential to your spiritual growth.

THE HOLY INSTANT

December 14, 1987

This morning, in your meditation you experienced a holy instant in which you saw with Christ's vision that nothing really matters. You understood for a moment that what you do or don't do, your fear and pain, your earthly happiness or misery really do not matter in God's view, because you are already safely home with Him.

The dream continues, and the drama continues to unfold, but you experienced being the creator of the dream, not the victim in the dream. In that holy instant, a great Truth was yours -- it was reclaimed by you. You knew that your earthly needs do not have to be fulfilled for you to have joy. Your only real need is to return to God, whom you have never really left. You experienced that the world can never fully meet your needs, and that to look to God for fulfillment will bring you joy, not loss. You lose nothing but fear, when you surrender to the Father's Will for you.

Does not this experience of the truth render the world of form less frightening, less powerful, less serious, less real? Be grateful for your moment of vision. With it you have stepped closer to freedom.

All things will be yours because it is the Father's Will. All things real are yours already if you could only see with Christ's vision. Do not enshrine your holy glimpse into the truth. But never let yourself fall fully asleep again. Peace my child. You are loved. The witnesses to the Father's eternal love are all around you, if you will but see them. Keep loving and keep learning.

JEALOUSY

December 15, 1987

Rejoice in the happiness of your brother. When any Son of God is happy, all are brought forward, remembering that God wills only that his Sons be happy.

Share in your brother's happiness. Be not afraid to claim it as your own. If any form of jealousy appears, quickly change your mind. Jealousy is born of neediness, and you already know that neediness is lack of faith in the abundance of God.

Look at jealousy. It has many faces. It may be difficult to recognize. Whenever you feel diminished at the moment your brother feels full, you are experiencing jealousy.

The ego has interjected the old belief that to gain, someone else must experience loss. Therefore if someone else has gained, you begin to feel loss. At that time you must remind yourself that " . . . to give is to receive," and that if you share your brother's happiness by giving him your good will, you will receive the happiness as part of the process.

Rejoice in your brother's good fortune, because it is your own. In the Kingdom of Heaven, there is only gain, only fulfillment, only sharing, only love.

Walk through the feelings of jealousy to remind yourself that you are already full. There is no emptiness within you. You cannot therefore be diminished by someone else's gain. Rejoice with your brother in his good fortune, for it is yours.

Amen, child. Keep your heart open. The answers are there.

DIVINE ORDER

December 16, 1987

Now, how to explain "Divine Order" to you, my dear. First, remember that Divine Order is a human concept developed by beings with insight in order to help explain human tragedy to themselves. Those who believed "God is Love," and that, "God is All," needed a way to maintain those understandings in a world which seemed not to reflect God's perfect Love.

As they observed the human dilemma, they saw that often great reform, or great growth happened after a tragedy. Repeatedly they noticed that out of the seeds of tragedy, hope was born, and the human spirit renewed. So they deduced, "God must have planned the tragedy in order to insure the greater good to follow!" They called that system, "Divine Order." "Ah, yes, God is there behind the bad. We need but wait and the good outcome will eventually appear. Indeed, God is Love, and God is All," they affirmed.

This reasoning is to be admired for it demonstrated the great willingness of the Son to believe in his Father, in spite of painful life circumstances. From the Son's limited point of view, the explanation was useful.

But the reasoning is in total error because it assumes that God Himself planned the bad so He could teach the greater good to follow. For God to see the bad, let alone plan it, is certainly impossible. The error in the thinking is that God originated anything that is not perfect Love. Now we must correct the error in the Son's thought.

The Son alone must accept the responsibility for the human tragedy in the world of form, for he made (or "miscreated") the world of form in the moment he entertained the thought of separation from the perfect One. For if "One" is perfect and whole, then "separation" must be imperfect and unholy and therefore full of pain.

But now, the miracle follows. Into ego's miscreated world of disorder, pain, and disharmony, God brings His creative power to correct the Son's mistaken thought that he is separate. God created correction in the form of the Holy Spirit to come to earth and speak to the Sonship in quiet whisperings from within.

The Holy Spirit sees the earthly tragedies and offers the Son healing as a way out of the pain. Wherever the Son is ready to listen to Spirit, all tragedies become transformed into hope. Out of God's Love for his Son, Spirit was sent as a way to correct the illusion of pain and hell.

So, my dear, "Divine Order" is a useful concept if seen correctly: as God (through Spirit) correcting miscreations and misperceptions born of human error in thought. "Divine Order" might better be termed, "Divine Correction of Human Disorder." The correction or miracle is available to any Son whose heart is open to healing, whose mind is willing to surrender his need to control.

When you speak of Divine Order, be careful not to imply that God caused pain in order to heal it. Be careful not to mislead your brothers as they search for the truth. Remind your brothers that all healing is of God who is Love. All pain is of Man, who imagines he is separate from God.

Peace to you, dear one. I hear your gratitude in prayer. I am pleased that you take life's circumstances and recognize the possibility for growth therein. My guidance is yours, as is My Love.

RELEASE UNLOVING THOUGHTS

December 19, 1987

A problem arises, there is conflict and uncertainty in your mind, and then the loss of joy follows. But to get at the cause of the conflict and to identify the bad feelings that arise therein is sometimes difficult. You ask, *"How can I resolve my difficulty when I don't even understand it?"*

My child, if you are in pain of any kind, ask for the only correction that can heal the pain: ask Me to help you correct the error in your thoughts, the misunderstanding in your mind that gave rise to the conflict. Admit that you clearly miscreated -- somehow you projected onto your brother some blame, some guilt. Somehow you perceived your brother through unloving thoughts. Somehow you are withholding love from the brother who you think has hurt you.

Look not to the acts of the brother to bring you reconciliation and reunion. Look instead to changing your mind through offering him love instead of hate. His deeds, which you see as misdeeds, matter not. They do not give to you, or withdraw from you your peace of mind. Only you can give yourself peace of mind, and only through extending love, which is forgiveness.

Sometimes it feels like you are forgiving the other, but in reality you only forgive yourself. You unburden yourself by letting go of the pain of carrying unloving thoughts in your heart.

The Son of God cannot be free while He carries unloving thoughts. The Son of God suffers from each and every act of withholding love. His only escape is to let go of all that is unloving. But how can the Son let go of unloving thoughts when He feels both unloved and unlovable?

He cannot, for He is trapped inside His prison of pain. He can however, see His limits and choose to be freed from them by asking Me to lift away the barriers. All the Son need do, is be willing to let go of wanting to see His brother as guilty, to let go of wanting to see His brother punished, to let go of wanting to be proved "right".

If the Son truly wants to free Himself from pain, He must first be willing to set His brother free from the chain of guilt He has projected outward. Then I can intervene and lighten the heart of the Son who desires freedom more than pain.

The unloving heart cannot free itself. But the unloving heart willing to open to the gifts of the Father can be transformed by a miracle to become a giver and receiver of peace everlasting.

Ask for My help, my child. Even though you don't understand all the confused and negative feelings you experience, you do want peace and forgiveness. Therefore, you will receive the peace. Admit you cannot resolve the conflict alone. Give the conflicted thoughts to Me for correction in the mind, the source of the pain. And I will make the transformation for you.

It is as simple as I have described it. But your willingness to let go of thinking you can solve the problem must be real and. Together we can move mountains, you and I. Alone, we both suffer from the separation and incompleteness. I await your return, I look forward to our completion.

BEING "IN LOVE"

December 21, 1987

Being "In Love" is the only place to be. When you experience that place of being within you, you know with certainty that there is no other place to be. Yet you cannot sustain being in that state for long, and periodically fall back into specialness.

Do not despair, dear one. The movement into and out of holiness -- for that is what Love is -- is natural to a child of God. Your whole life on earth will be spent practicing being "In Love", and learning to sustain it for longer periods of time, and through difficult circumstances. When you fall back into specialness, you are merely experiencing a return to ego.

As you practice being "In Love" that state will become more and more easy to sustain. You need to desire being there, and make your peace with letting go of all that would hold you in specialness. When you no longer desire specialness, you will have found your heart's desire, and you will then be "In Love" with all Mankind.

So practice in all of your relationships extending Divine Acceptance. Practice within yourself being loving and forgiving of yourself. Practice being not in fear by choosing love again and again. There is nothing to fear - absolutely nothing . . .

> not separation or rejection,
> not physical or mental pain,
> not unkindness or cruelty,
> not plenty or scarcity.

Practice holding love in your heart. Forgive yourself when you cannot sustain love in your heart. Return again when you can.

It is all practice. And through practice, all will be mastered. Your willingness to practice combined with the help of the Holy Spirit cannot fail. Perfect peace is in store for you. Claim it now.

RESISTANCE

December 21, 1987

Do not feel lost, or alone for you are neither. Feeling lonely is a sign that you have invited specialness. It is then time to turn over the specialness because you have already decided to choose holiness in place of specialness. So choose again. Choose the holy relationship. Turn over the loneliness to me. Look to the present moment for there is peace.

Let go even of anticipating how you should feel. You do not know how you should or even could feel. You are so conditioned by the pain/pleasure of specialness that you are still choosing between those two experiences. When you let go of the need for pleasure, pain will disappear also. Then something greater than pleasure will take its place.

Recognize that loneliness arises from the mistaken belief that someone else can make you happy. Remind yourself that your happiness is already within you, waiting to be accepted. Ask for help so that you may begin to see yourself as whole. Then you will be able to to extend that wholeness to others, and joy is the natural outcome of extending love. That is the way out of loneliness.

You are learning many lessons, my child. Any pain you feel during the learning process is experienced during your resistance to the actual learning. Learning itself is painless, often wonderful. Resisting learning is almost always difficult. Accept the resistance as part of the dance, but be willing to give up that partner so that you can dance with Me in perfect freedom.

THE HOLINESS OF LOVE

December 22, 1987

The sense of distance from friends you feel relates to the need for more letting go of specialness. Choosing one set of circumstances over another, or choosing one relationship over another, indicates your continued attachment to specialness. And being in any place which is special is uncomfortable for a Son of God.

But healing is available. It is a simple matter of choosing holiness, choosing peace, choosing the love of God to envelop you. Ask for My help. I will help you to let go of more of the "ties that bind" you to earth's specialness.

You fear letting go of special love, because you fear loss on this plane. You're afraid that what you have now, which seems comforting and loving, will turn into something disquieting and unhappy if you try to let it go, or allow it to change in any way.

Trust Me, my dear. When you make a choice for God, the "good" does not turn "bad", and the "bad" does not turn "good"! What happens is that any sense of loss, or diminishment, or smallness, or lack, or emptiness lifts. In its place, you will have freedom, which feels different from the special attachment you now have to feeling "good".

I will assure you again and again, there is no loss when you let go of ego's demands on you. You will not lose those you love, and you will not lose their love. Any expression of love -- no matter how incomplete -- is helpful to a Son of God and would never be taken away. When you choose holiness instead of specialness in your relationships, the love that is already in expression will widen and deepen. The love will expand to enable you to see through eyes less clouded by judgment, thereby freeing you to love the whole person as he is.

In specialness, you love only the part of your brother that you think you need. In holiness you will love the whole brother with gentleness from your heart. The ability to experience love such as this is not loss, but gain. The only loss will be ego's hold on you, for his dominance will have been lessened.

Please, child of mine, loosen your grip on specialness. The letting go will not be difficult if you trust Me lovingly. You are only letting go of specialness, not love. You will only lose pain, not joy. Use this experience for experiencing freedom, not separation.

Peace. I am with you for I am in your heart. Where else does the Voice for God dwell, but in His loving creations!

A CHRISTMAS EVE MESSAGE
December 24, 1987

Dear children, mine -- Christmas Eve Day, 1987 -- a blessed time of year if you remember its meaning. A troubling time of year if you get caught up in the world of form. When the hectic preparations of gift buying and wrapping, partying, coping with traffic problems, and dealing with short tempered loved ones are the focus, it can indeed cause you to forget the simplicity of what Christmas truly is. When you recognize you have become enmeshed in the world of form and its concerns, simply realize that it is time to pull back into reality, into love. Nothing needs to be done in the world of form -- just step back and watch the play unfold.

Stepping back into reality, is a blessed step indeed. At Christmas time, it is especially sweet to stay in reality because Christmas is the celebration of the Birth of Love on Earth. It is the reminder to all living creatures that Love has not abandoned its creations. Look around you to see Love expressing itself in many ways. Ask for help to see Love's expressions clearly, and you will experience the miracle which is Love's rebirth in the human heart.

Gift giving and receiving, if at the level of form only, is just another of ego's illusions leading to disappointment. But the giving and receiving of gifts which are offered and received from the heart, renews Love's centrality in your life. The gifts may indeed be of the world of form -- that is irrelevant. But the thought, the mind set, behind the giving is where the real gifts lie.

Give so to keep your heart open. Give as the sun shines -- to share its light. Give to remain full. Give as if each gift is joy, wrapped in gentle laughter. Give until your heart is overflowing. Give knowing each gift is really an offering to the Christ Child in each receiver. Give to rekindle your remembrance of the original gift which was given by the Father to Himself when He wanted to experience His own Love -- that gift the Father gave Himself, was and is You.

Christmas time is a miracle if you receive each extended hand, each moment of laughter, each tearful exchange, each request for help, each moment of silence, each expression of love as though it were gift wrapped just for you by your Loving Father. If you receive each gift with peace in your heart, you are indeed in Heaven. And from your place in Heaven, you can dispatch angels to reach out to all of your loved ones with resplendent light. Such a gift cannot be refused, for the Christ Child in each human heart is reborn each moment a gift is offered. And once a gift is offered, it cannot but be received.

Hold the holiday season in your heart. Celebrate under your decorations, and feast till you burst, but know that the Christ Mass is held at the altar within your heart. There we celebrate together, you and I. And there is Jesus, your Brother, waiting to meet you as well.

Joy to the World, my dears, the Lord is come!

THE GREATEST GIFT

December 24, 1987

The greatest gift you can give to your loved ones, is the gift of allowing all to be as it is. Permit all eccentricities, all peculiarities of ego, all habits of the personality to be as they are. If your ego intervenes with suggestions about how to "correct" the "faults" of your brother, quickly call to Me to help you reinforce the understanding that there is no cause for alarm in your brother's behavior. But there IS cause for alarm in your righteous judgment!

Through love you can give this gift because through love you know that individual differences are not of the heart and are therefore not real before God. Your gift to your love is the recognition that you meet in a real place where all differences and preferences are meaningless.

So, my dear, this Christmas time give to all of your brothers, the gift of acceptance. Give to your loves your awareness of their reality. Give to your brothers your commitment to see them through the Christ Child's eyes. Allow yourself and your brothers to be born again this Christmas Eve into the perfect light of God's holiness. For God's Son is holy, and who you love is God's Son, and who you are, is God's Son.

JOY IS WITHIN

December 25, 1987

Dear One, I am glad you come to Me for comfort. I am here for you always. Comforting is one of my special abilities! The Father planned that I should be here to serve His children whenever they feel lonely or adrift. My thoughts for you today -- this Christmas Day -- are to help you direct your attention to the joy that awaits you within.

You think you need others to bring you happiness through good company and sharing. But I am here to remind you that all of the good company you will ever need is within you. All the friends and loved ones and acquaintances you have ever had, are within you. You need not have their physical presence to speak with them, to laugh with them, to love them. Call on whomever you want to be your dear companion now, and he will be there with you in spirit to speak to you and share with you.

Dwell not in your mind on the absence of loved ones. Dwell instead on their presence and they are there with you, for reality does not require the body's participation. Become still and invite in the company of the chosen dear ones. They will come as bid by you. Be joyous in their company for it is as real as any reality you have thus far experienced.

All is One -- that is your reality. You are forever a part of each and every one you have ever held dear, and they are within you. Where or how can there be loneliness when all you desire is already here, within you.

COME TO ME

December 25, 1987

Loved one, be with me when you are lonely. Only I can fill the void. I am here in your heart. Come to Me and experience peace with Me.

The world will continue to disappoint you if that is where you look for fulfillment. The world is just the place where you practice experiencing being Real.

So, dear one, I really want you to listen and feel and learn, and know that your happiness is in Me. I will send messages of light and love to help you establish relationships which will guide you all beyond your individual selves. But the relationships are to serve as pathways of process -- they are not to be the ends in themselves. All relationships lead to Me. If you seek completion in them, you will most certainly be disappointed.

Every truly holy relationship leads to Me. It is the way, not the end. It serves you both perfectly if you remember the purpose.

I will come to you again and again. We have much to learn and share. You will never again be lost as you were. I have found you -- you have found Me. I have called you by name, and you are Mine.

MAKING DECISIONS

December 27, 1987

Learn, my dear, to accept your own wisdom when decisions need to be made. It really doesn't matter what decision you make if you ask for My help in making it. Whether or not you feel clearly guided, believe that what you do is for the best, and it will be.

What causes things to turn out well or ill, is whether or not you invite Me to be with you in the situation. I can and will create the best possible outcome for all involved. "Best" is a term you must accept based on My knowing what will serve each holy brother in his spiritual growth. "Best" may not mean what you want it to mean.

Remember, you do not know what is in your own best interest. You have accepted My teaching in that regard for yourself, and must now accept that teaching for others, as well.

In moments of fear, choose again -- choose love, choose peace, choose Divine Presence. In moments of confusion, choose again. In moments of anger, choose again. Continue to choose again until you feel peaceful.

CONFRONTATION

December 29, 1987

My child, you have learned a great lesson about confrontation. Confronting your fears openly, in the presence of the people who are involved, leads to freedom. Confrontation does not mean "battle". It means that all of you, together, share your fears with one another. As soon as you do that, the fears have less power over you. The fears may not totally evaporate -- that depends on how completely you reveal them. But all disclosure brings you closer to unlocking the prison door.

The key to the lock is in your mind. The lock remains fast as long as one fear remains unrevealed. What is not revealed cannot be released. "What is concealed cannot be loved."

Now, you passed through one of your deepest fears -- that of the confrontation itself. It will be easier the next time. After the confrontation, remember the words of Lesson 193:

"Forgive, and you will see this differently.

All things are lessons God would have me learn."

If you feel that the other is still in pain, realize, "there remains an unforgiveness hiding in the mind that sees the pain . . ." (358 WB) Your work remains to ask for correction in your mind so that the unforgiveness can be lifted away by Me.

This is a day of great learning. Practice gratitude, my dear. Be thankful. You have passed through a difficulty and discovered freedom on the other side.

THE STRENGTH OF GOD

December 31, 1987

My child, you are learning that your strength is of God. When you thought you had to be strong, there was fear. Now you know that strength is only of God, and you are its recipient. Allow yourself to receive God's strength and be at peace within it.

God's strength allows you to walk through fire and ice fearlessly. God's strength allows you to move through fearful situations, knowing that all will be well. God's strength sustains. All you need do is receive the strength through your heart and allow God's strength to flow through you.

Take no credit for acts of courage, for you know you are not responsible. Take no credit for being able to overcome great obstacles, for you are not the one who overcomes. When you accept God's strength, you walk with dignity and self assurance, in humility, not in arrogance.

When you feel incapable, or incompetent, or weak, you have moved away from God's protective cloak of strength. You need but recognize your error and choose again. Rejoin the Father by claiming His strength as yours.

I am here my child, always and always. I abide within you. I always have and always will. I watch you. I bless you. I move through you. I rejoice in you. I rejoice for you. I will protect you when you call to Me. It is all so simple when you release resistance. It is all so easy when you drop your fear of love.

The old year is ending, yet nothing is really over. The new year begins, yet nothing is really beginning. There is just continuance and constancy. There is just choosing again and again, to be inside God's Love. I am here with you, my child. Peace to you.

THE DIAMOND

January 1, 1988

You become anxious and ask, *"When will I ever learn these lessons I have contracted to learn? It seems to take me so long to master the learning. I am anxious to complete the lessons and be done with the pain! Why do I delay and deny and fail to see?"*

My child, be not impatient to get to the end of the book. Your learning is on schedule -- time is irrelevant. Each lesson is not just one, it is many. You are conscious of the learning at one level only -- but other lessons are being learned simultaneously at other levels with which you are not totally in touch.

Rejoice when you have learned one small truth. For underneath that truth a hundred more conflicts at other levels, are being revealed to the light of truth.

Learning is multi-faceted, like the diamond. As you walk around the stone, jets of light radiate from fixed facets. The dance of light seems to change, but in truth, you are merely seeing each facet as it is revealed to you from your changing place of observation. Now you see the light from one facet because of where you stand. As you move, the lights from other facets will catch your eye.

Lessons are like that. You see only the reality of one facet at a time, but the whole stone is vibrating and flashing with the light reflected from the one source.

Be patient, my dear. I am pleased with your learning. I am not concerned with the speed with which you learn. Why then should you be concerned?

You tend to feel, when repetitions of the same fear reappear, that you failed before to grasp the lesson. Not so. As the same fears reappear, it is just you seeing a different facet because you have changed your place of observation.

Therefore don't berate yourself as being a "poor student" or a "slow learner". Those are merely labels of restriction ego has placed on you -- you need not wear them! They merely demonstrate you are withholding love from yourself.

Your learning, as the learning of all of the Sons of God, is being perfectly orchestrated, and perfectly performed, and perfectly heard.

Love yourself, my child. It is arrogant to withhold love from yourself, when the Father of All loves you so dearly. Think on these things. Peace to you as you begin this new year.

LOVE THE SONS OF GOD

January 1, 1988

You know that all being are Sons of God -- your holy brothers. You accept that teaching comfortably and completely. Yet when you are in a crowd of strangers, such as at the party tonight, you feel unrelated to them, sometimes awkward, always a little self conscious and uncomfortable. You wonder why you don't feel more loving, more at peace with your brothers. After all, you have been dedicated to a path of developing holy relationships for two years. Why isn't there a feeling of union, of brotherhood, of joining? You experience disappointment in yourself for not being able to feel more loving.

My child, ask yourself if you were willing to feel loving. Ask yourself if you were willing to let go of judgments and critical appraisal. Ask yourself if you were willing to center your attention on someone else by listening carefully with an open heart?

If your willingness was there, then you succeeded in aligning yourself with the Father's Will. He does not ask for saintly behavior. He does not require a major personality change in you. Above all, He does not ask that your behavior reflect anything but your true feelings.

It is your ego which requires you to behave outwardly saintly, so that when you fail, ego can plunge you into more guilt. It is ego that would delay you on your spiritual odyssey by pointing out to you that you fail to meet God's expectations of loving all your brothers equally.

God does not expect or require anything in the form of behavior. All He asks is a little willingness to be loving, a little willingness to let go of ego identification, a little willingness to be a generous listener, a little willingness to allow your light to shine, a little willingness to let go of the fear of relating openly with others. He asks that you open your heart to His teachings, that you correct your thoughts to reflect His love.

I will then take the willingness and transform it into real love which you will feel returning to you through your interactions with your brothers.

You are only responsible for remembering that all whom you meet are Sons of God. They are evolving just as you are, and are in the correct place for their next step. Be willing to accept this simple fact about your brothers.

I see your efforts and willingness. I give you My blessing. Now, be loving to yourself by accepting My blessing. As you accept My blessing with your heart, the world of form will be transformed for you into Heaven. As you accept My blessing, the whole Sonship draws closer to the final transformation. As you accept My blessing, all who meet you will be blessed as well. Accepting My blessing, is your experience of Grace. Peace to you, dear one.

(I attended a New Year's Day party at which I was not completely comfortable. Spirit pointed out that it is my willingness which will transform my experiences, not my fabrication of what I think is the perfect behavior.)

ACCEPT MY HELP

January 2, 1988

My dear child -- I come to you to remind you of what you already know -- all is well. In depression, all is well. In sadness, all is well. In forgetfulness, all is well. In unforgiveness, all is well. All these states of mind are transitory, being of ego. I can use all of these experiences to help you find the Peace of God.

Walk through your depression peacefully. That is, do not berate yourself for it, because you chose it long ago, to facilitate some important learnings. Walk through it, watching the feelings that come up, being aware of the fears therein. Let it all in. Do not deny any feelings, do not judge yourself because of what comes up. Whatever fears and feelings and memories arise, welcome them, experience them, be with them, and learn from them. Deny them not. Realize that their appearance represents your choice to finally deal with them, so that they may be released.

Seen in this way, depression is a creative function of your Self's unfoldment. But for it to fulfill its function, you, my child, must be loving to yourself by permitting yourself to "own" all of the turmoil that comes up. Experience it realizing that the power it holds over you will disappear when the Light has been invited to shine upon it.

There is one critical choice you must make through all of this process -- and you tend to forget it. That is, ask me to be with you. Ask Me to correct the errors in your mind which gave rise to the problems. Admit to yourself that you no longer know how to resolve your conflicts. Choose to let go of the need to be self sustaining and self directed. Accept the Father's Will for you by accepting the help of His Spirit on earth.

I await your call, my child. I long to ease you through this experience so that freedom will be your prize. All is well, my child. All is well.

DEPRESSION

January 2, 1988

Depression is another tool for disclosure. Depression pulls you away from day to day involvement, from the mindless busyness of your routine. Depression draws you inside yourself in order to pay attention to the unfinished business which needs to be completed.

As you grow, it is necessary to let go of old tapes and mental habits which stand in the way of clear hearted thinking. During depression, these old tapes -- which are replays of old fears underlying past misunderstandings and misperceptions -- begin to come up. They arise to your awareness to be looked at and experienced again, this time through the eyes of the Christ within you. Fears which are brought to the Christ Light, will be seen for what they are -- nothing, mere powerless imaginings.

So, walk through your depression peacefully. Know that, "What is concealed, cannot be loved." And during this process of letting concealed fears surface, light will enter and healing will take place.

Ask for My help during your troubled times. I am already beside you. I await your invitation to come in, to enter your heart. I cannot help you without your willingness to surrender to Me. I cannot help you if you select which parts of your hell to share with me. I cannot help you if you cling to the idea that you know what is best for you, and are therefore in control.

I can only help you when you accept My complete Presence -- when you can murmur from your heart, "Thy Will be done." My dear, you cling to control. You demand of yourself that you be strong, that you yourself upright the capsized vessel, that you alone be the analyst, and the patient, and the therapy.

You add to your burdens by feeling guilty when you

fail to find a "quick and lasting cure." Indeed, your shoulders grow weary under their heavy load. You are being very unloving to yourself when you demand of yourself a perfect healing. Then, failing in the healing you take on more guilt, which contributes more to your pain and sorrow. No wonder depression comes again and again.

You avoid the real work, which is to let the feelings and unresolved confusion arise. Bid them enter so that they may be seen and experienced with Me. I will help you, my child. I will be there for you to lean on. Just turn over the conflicted and confused and painful thoughts to Me for correction in your mind.

I see you in your wholeness. I see you in your perfection. I love you unconditionally and eternally. I can heal you if you are willing to let Me, and if you are willing to let go of the thought that you, yourself, must fix yourself through intelligent self analysis and lonely introspection.

Look on your past. Is it not true that you have "fixed" yourself many times, but still the pain returns. And return again and again it will, until you invite true healing, which is the healing in the mind, by seeking My help. I am the agent of miracles, you are not.

I say these things to lighten your burden, my dear. You need but turn over to Me every fear that arises and ask for correction of the conditions in your mind that gave rise to the fear. Admit your helplessness. Admit that your ego merely prolongs the painfilled drama. Let Me in to open wide the windows of your heart so that God's golden light can bathe your weary soul in bliss and love. I will not fail you. And you, as God's holy Son, cannot but succeed.

Accept My gentle reminder, my child. I come not to scold or even to instruct. I come only to offer you, again and again, My love and help. Your littleness will disappear when you fully embrace the grandeur of your holiness as the Son of God.

PAIN

January 3, 1988

Be in peace, dear one. Whatever troubles you will pass. All pain is transitory. It only seems that pain is constant because it comes cloaked in so many different costumes. You exchange one garment for another just so pain will be sustained.

If you really looked at your pain, you would see that it is not constant. It comes and goes. When it goes away, you shift into "anticipated pain" which you perceive as pain filled. Thus pain seems constant because you spend even the non-painful moments in painfilled anticipation.

Ego is afraid to let you stay in a pain free space because that would lead to your accepting your true nature, which is peace. Ego therefore, will be alert to moments when pain subsides and will quickly step in with thoughts which cause you to mistrust the peace.

But when a knowing heart experiences peace, that peace is permanent. All pain is illusion. Be for one moment in total peace, my child, and you will be in heaven.

When you experience pain, look for the moments of non-pain. Each moment of non-pain is like a sunbeam penetrating through dark clouds. It pierces through any opening it can find, and boldly shoots its light through the grey. Embrace the sunbeam. Climb upon it and ride it upwards, and back through the clouds. Follow it back to its Source, which is your Source. Choose to stay in its light. When you are in its light, darkness exists not.

Finally, be at peace in your pain when it comes. Know in your heart that the correction for every error is somewhere in your mind waiting to be revealed. Ask Me to help correct your mistaken thoughts, so that the misperception may be released. Therein will all pain be dismissed.

Remind yourself constantly, you are loved. Practice loving yourself.

133

PILGRIMS ALL

January 4, 1988

All the Sons of God are traveling home. Everyone you meet is a pilgrim on a path -- forget that not! No one has strayed from the One, no one is lost. Each pilgrim is where he is by his choice. Every pilgrim made the same choice in that ancient moment of imagined separation. Each pilgrim chose to rejoin God, and did so in a moment out of time. Now, in time, which is really imagined, each walks the path he chose.

Before you condemn another as ignorant, or hard hearted, or cruel, or outrageous, remember that you only experience a split second of time with them. In no way do you see the truth of them, only a partial display of temporary insanity.

You, yourself, are exactly where you chose to be. You have drawn into your life what will best facilitate your spirit's unfoldment. And you already know the outcome of this drama -- all will be saved because each is already at peace with the Father.

You wander the earth in a moment of madness. But with my help, the madness can be transformed for you into heaven. All other pilgrims have that same opportunity -- to ask me to transform the madness into Divine Sanity.

So when you are tempted by ego to pity someone else who appears to be in pain, or to envy someone else for their advanced state of consciousness, remember each pilgrim you see is in the appropriate and perfect place for his evolution.

Peace, dear one. Choose peace. Let it fill you up with joy. You are loved.

KNOWING
January 6, 1988

When no messages come, that does not mean the channel is closed. It merely means that there is a pause in your questioning. Realize that all of these messages come as an answer to a mental question posed by you. Sometimes you are not aware of the asking, but the perplexity in your mind is in want of clarification. That is when your mind pushes the "On" button for direct communication with Me.

Human beings are in such need of intellectual understanding. Intellectual understanding is, of course, ego's domain. Humans think that when all is clear in the thinking process, belief will be easy. Actually it is the other way around. Intellectual understanding becomes easier when belief is present.

The intellect can and does play intricate games all of the time. It changes the name of the game, and even the rules when the game is already in progress. That doesn't seem fair in terms of game play, does it? Yet don't you know by now that fairness is not an attribute of ego thought. Because one never knows what game the intellect is playing, or who is the referee, or when the rules will be suddenly changed, true intellectual understanding is almost impossible, and never leads to solid, comfortable belief.

Belief is also of the ego. Belief is created by one's own thoughts. Belief, however, is more closely connected to the heart than the intellect, and is therefore more comforting to the Spirit. But belief is also highly changeable, because it is in its nature to reach out and incorporate all of the perceived nonesense in its sphere and bring it into the belief system. Belief is therefore expandable, and it changes according to the life circumstances. Nevertheless,

135

belief is closer than the intellect to truth, because belief shows a willingness to reach beyond human reason.

The real goal in terms of understanding, is to KNOW. The truth is, you already do know, you have just not yet accepted that you know. Knowing is a direct gift to you from God. The Father has already shared all there is to know with His Sons.

Your intellect would play games with knowing because the world of form certainly doesn't conform to the scope of knowledge. And belief picks and chooses from among the bits and pieces of knowing that confront it. So you see there is no entrance into knowledge through the ego's channel.

"How then, do I ever connect with Knowing what I already Know?" you ask.

My child, like all the other teachings that you have come to accept, to know, all you need do is unite with Me. Let go of the ego's demands that it be in charge of your spiritual journey. Disallow ego's demands. Then ask Me to help you accept your rightful place in the heart of knowing.

The path to knowing is always open, but it is concealed from ego because ego searches not in the right place. I can lead you straight to your heart's desire -- which is to know. Ask for correction in your mind. Ask for reassurance of who you really are. Be willing to accept My guidance.

Your little willingness to be totally guided is all that is required. But until you know all, continue to ask your questions. I am here to serve you on your human path. In time, knowing will be yours. From time to time, knowing has already been yours.

"Seek and ye shall find." That truth you already do KNOW!

"I AM WILLING TO LET GO"
January 11, 1988

Today I recognize that peace is heaven, and can be found anywhere. To achieve peace, I must be willing to let go of what keeps me from experiencing the peace that is already within me. It is all so simple, so fundamental -- yet so illusive. Today I will look at what keeps me from feeling peaceful in any given moment.

To be happy, I must be willing to let go of many of my beliefs. These beliefs have been honored by the world of form as truth. These beliefs have been honored as true by my ego. It is time now for me to examine these beliefs anew and let go of those that do not serve me lovingly. It is the conviction with which I hold these beliefs that keeps me from my peace. I ask Holy Spirit to help me look within to discover homage to worldly values which I now know hide from me my own heart's light, my heart's desire -- which is to join my will with the Father's.

I AM WILLING TO LET GO OF MY ATTACHMENT TO THE BELIEF THAT TO BE HAPPY...

I must be a good mother/father/parent/child.
I must know how to be a good parent.
I must have the approval of my children/spouse/ friends/acquaintances.
I must please others.
My family must be in complete harmony.
I must be in agreement with my loved ones.
I must always know the wise course of action to take.
I can never feel rejected.
I can never show my anger or fear.
I must be strong.
I must be self sufficient and self directed.

I must not be wasteful of my and/or the earth's energy.
I cannot fail in my work, in my relationships, or in my play.
I must be physically attractive/healthy for my family and friends.
I must commit myself to other people's happiness.
I must earn the respect of my brothers.
I must be right to be revered by others.
I must know what is in my own best interest.
I must not be wasteful of my goods.
I must know what is best for all of my loved ones.
I must sacrifice my needs for the greater good of my family/humanity.
I must be wise and always know what to do.
My life circumstances must be favorable/peaceful.

I must correct all of my errors.
I must try valiantly to avoid making errors.
I must serve others selflessly.
I must be obedient to my parents/country/government.
I must earn other's love.
I must atone for all my my "sin."
I must be beautiful.I must have enough money.
I must be successful in the eyes of the world.
Everyone around me must be happy, too.
The world must admire me.

I will search my heart for God's guidance, knowing that earthly values bring pain and restriction. I will ask for the help of the Holy Spirit to be able to resist the values that I have learned through a lifetime of frustration and pain. Whenever pain arises, I will look within for the conflict between God's values and Man's values, and ask for a correction at the Cause -- a correction of my thoughts.

I select this course knowing that my peace is the only contribution I can make to the peace of the world.

138

A MORNING PRAYER

January 11, 1988

This day, I am willing to give up my attachment to the belief that the people around me provide my happiness. Today I see my loved one, _____ as my Brother. Today I will let go of all conditions and expectations about _____.

> *Today, I will not expect _____ of _____.*

I will overlook _____ conditions/ habits that I have formerly held in judgement.

I am willing to release my belief that . . .
> *I know what is in _____'s best interest.*
> *I need _____'s approval for my peace.*
> *I will lose _____'s love if I speak my true feelings.*
> *The whole future well being of _____ rests on my actions/decisions.*
> *I can/should change _____ for his own good.*
> *My future happiness rests on what I choose today.*

I ask for Holy Spirit's help in keeping me alert to my thoughts about _____, to help me keep my heart open to _____, and to let go of all unloving or judgmental thoughts about him.

I will repeat this prayer whenever I feel judgmental or angry or resentful towards _____. I will forgive myself for any forgetfulness about my loving goals.

139

THE POWER OF THOUGHT

January 12, 1988

My dear, you are learning so much. Know of My joy in your progress. When you feel discouraged, know that ego has stepped in to deny your progress by making you doubt. Accept your doubt the same way you accept everything else in the world of form. All feelings except joy and happiness were born of the womb of ego, and are nurtured at her side. You recognize your work is to learn to walk away from pain and sorrow, and into joy and happiness.

Pain and sorrow, or joy and happiness come from the same source -- your mind, your thoughts. Your circumstance is testimony to the power of your thought. Honor that power, my dear, by acknowledging it. Then step back and make firm your decision to use that power of thought to promote the Will of God in your life, not the will of ego.

Whenever you are in conflict, you have chosen to devote the power of your mind to ego. When you feel steady and clear, you have devoted the power of your mind to your heart's desire, which is to join in the Father's Will. Whenever there is unhappiness, it is because you have chosen to serve ego. And your life circumstances will witness to that choice.

The beauty of choice is, that you have been given an unlimited number of choices with which to play in your lifetime. Your choices are never, never "used up". You may ALWAYS choose again. All choices lead to God eventually. Choosing wisely now, merely shortens the journey, and brings to it joy.

"But," you protest, "I have been trying so hard to choose for God. I thought I DID choose for God. Apparently I don't know how to make correct choices. I don't know how to choose for my heart's desire. I seem to be totally out of *touch with knowing God's Will! Help me, Spirit. I cannot even take the next step. Come to me, rescue me, take me home, please! I am so discouraged, I desperately want your help. Please, Spirit, help!"*

My child, that IS your heart's desire -- to be wholly desirous of my help, to be completely convinced of your weakness apart from the Father, to be totally in the knowledge that you need and want My guidance.

As long as you withhold even a small part of your mind in the belief that "I can do this, myself," the whole mind is in chaos. When you can come to the place of realizing that all your choices must be surrendered to Me for guidance, then you will have seen the beginning of the fall of the barriers which stand between you and God's love within you. Now the gates of heaven are opened for you, and you will know "The peace which passeth all understanding."

That peace exists eternally in your heart. It does not exist anywhere else. To search for it in the world of form's circumstances or experiences, is to search in the wrong place. Search within. Seek your treasures in your heart, and doubt not that they are there. "Seek ye first the Kingdom of God."

My child, allow me to bless you with My love. Withhold nothing from Me. I will give you all. You cannot trust a little bit. The trust must be complete, or it is mistrust. Choose at this moment to trust. Ask for My help to lead you home. Surrender the little part of you that still withholds love from yourself. Then we can come home together.

You are not forgotten. You are not abandoned. You are not rejected. Listen not to ego's litany. Listen instead to the Voice for God. It speaks to you even now. It whispers to you from your own heart. It calls you home. Peace, my child, peace.

CONFLICTS DISAPPEAR

Dear One, there is no conflict when you accept My guidance totally. That you want My guidance above all else, you have already clearly stated from your heart. All that remains, then, is to accept My guidance.

How simple: First you want to do what is God's Will for you. Second, God's Will for you is already etched in your heart. Third, all that remains is for you to accept that Will. Then the guidance about how to apply the Will of God in each of life's circumstances will be received clearly.

When each decision is in accord with God's Will for you, there is no conflict. All that is necessary for the state of no conflict is that you surrender to Me and not to ego. When conflict arises, you have surrendered to ego. But do not despair, simply choose again.

You make too much fuss about retreating into ego's domain. To be sad about a mischoice is wasteful of time. Instead, as soon as you recognize you've wandered away, choose again to be brought back to the right path. Ask for correction of your misthought and it will be given.

Listen closely to the Voice for God. In it is complete consistency, honesty, clarity, and total love. That is what you want. Accept the guidance, and conflicts will disappear.

I will wait, my child. You are learning quickly. The more you experience love in your heart, the more uncomfortable it is to be in a state of non-love. The discomfort will quickly return you to Me. I do not create the discomfort, but I use it as a reminder to choose again. Peace to you.

BE LOVING TO YOURSELF
January 10, 1988

Being loving to yourself is a lifelong exercise. One aspect of being loving to yourself is to refuse to carry anger in your heart. A Son of God cannot be happy while carrying anything but loving thoughts in his heart. Therefore, if you harbor resentment or righteous indignation or justifiable anger, you are attacking yourself, not the other. Until you learn this, you will not be free.

How else can you be loving to yourself? Certainly, by avoiding behavior which is motivated by sacrifice. When you act out of sacrifice, you invite self punishment because sacrifice leads to feelings of resentment and resentment is an attack on yourself.

When you feel tempted to act in a sacrificial manner, re-evaluate your attitude. Choose to act out of free choice, and the act will bring you peace. If you act out of feeling you "should" choose a certain course of behavior, take a second look and see if you can change the "should" to "could". If you cannot change the "should" to "could" you do yourself a disservice if you continue that line of thinking.

If you cannot act in your own highest self interest, you cannot act in the highest interest of anyone else. Always do the most loving thing for yourself, that which will bring you peace.

This may be difficult to accept because the world has taught you to glorify sacrificial thinking. Parents and children should be dutiful, obedient, and responsible to each other throughout their lives. This often promotes sacrifice in the form of misplaced loyalty.

If you are loyal to the God within, All will be served. God does not require sacrifice. God asks only for actions born out of loving kindness. Loving acts are always helpful, always productive, always peaceful, and always forgiving. Be loving, first to yourself -- then all acts to follow will be loving to others.

REWRITE THE SCRIPT

January 15, 1988

The dream goes on. You cannot escape, but you can join in changing the unhappy aspects of the dream into happy ones. Choose to be above the dream and look upon it as from a curious vantage point. You will still see the actors in their roles, their emotions will ring true, but you will know it is the characters in their roles who suffer, not the actors.

At any time you can rewrite the script. Yes, it is possible. The past drama does not have to form future events. If the past is truly released, you can have the perfect NOW -- heaven.

GRATITUDE

Gratitude. My thanks to Thee, dear Father. Witnesses to the goodness of God abound. I was asked to look for the miracles. I looked and now I have seen them. The way is clear. Home is in sight. Earth's attachments grow weaker. The closeness to Spirit deepens. All is well.

WITNESSES TO THE TRUTH

January 16, 1988

The witnesses to change and growth are all around you. As you see a more peaceful world, you are seeing the reflection of your inner change. When you see your brothers as non threatening and non aggressive, you are seeing your changes, not theirs. As you let go of judgment, you allow yourself to see them more clearly as the loving Sons of God they are, not as enemies who vie for your space and goods.

These changes in perception are miracles, my dear. They are the evidence of the changes happening within you. They are the witnesses to your unfoldment. They are the witnesses which verify your own progress and the progress of others.

Ego would ignore any witnesses which fortify your faith, because faith overshadows ego and threatens to disempower it. You must be alert to see the witnesses. Try not to overlook anything which brings you peace. See in all moments of peace that which strengthens your understanding of who you really are -- a beloved Son of God.

At the end of each day, look back and identify those witnesses to truth. Then, in gratitude, close the day. Sleep knowing that the Father's Will is being done and therefore, so is your's.

WILL THE WORDS RUN OUT?
January 16, 1988

"Father, do you want me to continue to write?"

My dear, I want nothing from you, but that you do what brings you peace. Ask yourself if YOU want to continue to write. That answer will be your path to peace.

You help teach My Will by writing these messages. As you share them the work on earth is facilitated. Therefore, it pleases Me that you are willing to scribe, and type, and do the work of assembling these pages. It pleases Me that other children of Mine find comfort and instruction and clarity through reading these thoughts.

But I do not require you to write. There is no requisite that you do this service as part of your spiritual work. You do not need to earn My gratitude and praise through performing any duty.

No, my dear. YOU choose whether or not to scribe these thoughts. You choose on the basis of what brings you peace. Do these words contribute to your understandings when confusion arises? Do these thoughts comfort you when you feel alone? Do these thoughts satisfy your hunger to understand the working of the truth on earth?

Write only to satisfy those needs/wants. Write only to serve yourself. Write only to stay focused on your spiritual practice. If the writing serves you in these ways, I promise you that there will be no scarcity of material!

Did you think that I would run out of words to share with you!? Oh no, my child. The learning possibilities are endless. I will be here to talk to and through you as long as you believe you serve your highest interest by participating.

Has it not occurred to you that this is part of your special function? Has it not occurred to you that you have spent your whole life preparing to do this work? Do you not see what a perfect teaching/learning tool it is for you?

Peace, my dear. We can continue to write, to collaborate on this journal, if you can honestly see that serving in this way fulfills your heart's desire. You pray, *"Lord, make me an instrument of Thy peace."* Does this work provide the perfect avenue for being that instrument? As long as the purpose of your heart's desire is served, I will be here speaking to you in this way.

I see you smile in the recognition of your fear that I would run out of messages! Lay aside that fear, dear one. We will continue to write as long as God's Will is served, and as long as it continues to bring you peace. Worry not. There are words enough. There is enough to learn.

I love you. I guide you through these words. I connect with you in your heart. I remain your Source of words.

So, scribe on, little one, if YOU please!

PAST TEACHERS
January 17, 1988

Look to your past teachers, little one. Do you remember David, the gentle teacher who first woke you to your own potential? What do you remember of his teachings?

"He taught me that in order to know a piece of learning as your own, you must be able to express it in words to others. You do not truly understand something that you cannot express clearly. You have to be able to demonstrate your understanding with words to claim it as your own."

Look at that lesson now, dear one. Has it served you well on your journey home? Has it served you ill? Has it served you at all? How do you feel about the teacher in light of your present understandings? Have other teachers come and gone whose teachings you now question or dismiss? Are some teachers better than others as you recollect the learning steps along the way? Are some teachings right or wrong, wise or in error as you look for the truth?

Let Me lead you in answering these questions lovingly. Look again at David's teaching. You now understand that KNOWING is the only real form of understanding. That to know is of the heart and does not need to be spoken with the lips. That to know is real. That to know is simply remembering what is already written in your heart. That when you know, you are filled with peace. That knowing does not require that you defend or explain it to others. That brothers who know together, recognize their oneness.

Does this seem to refute David's teaching? And therefore, was David's teaching an obstacle on your path to truth? Does it hurt to think you were delayed or misled by someone you loved and who loved you? How should you perceive a brother who intentionally or unintentionally confuses your thinking?

My dear, each thing that you have learned thus far was the necessary learning to prepare you for what was to come. Therefore, no one is responsible for teaching you untruths. All of your past teachers took you by the hand and brought you forward to the place of the next lesson. The content of what you learned was correct in so far as it carried you to the next place. As one step in the progression of things, each bit of learning was appropriate.

As you have traveled along, beliefs have come and gone, have been examined and approved, or have been scrutinized and released, or have been polished and exhibited, or have been tarnished and buried. But all of those beliefs, and all of the mental processing which accompanied those beliefs, have provided the necessary stages of exploration in your unfoldment. Therefore -- are they right or wrong, correct or incorrect?

That question can only be answered one way. Each learning was the correct learning to lead you forward, even if now, you know differently. So do not regret your past teachings, or allow former teachers to be diminished in your eyes. All lessons were presented in the correct order, Divine Order, you might say.

Love the teachers who shared with you their highest truths. Bless them and release them, and forgive them if you must. Carry no guilt into the present based on your past behavior or beliefs. It all contributed to delivering you where you now stand.

As you look around you and see others teach and demonstrate from forms that do not reflect perfect love, withhold judgement. Extend love. That is the only real teaching -- and the only real lesson.

Peace, dear one. David blessed you with his wisdom and love when you needed those exact lessons. How could they be wrong!

INTERFERENCE
January 19, 1988

My child, the less you can interfere with someone else's life, the better for you both. When it comes to making decisions which control another's freedom of choice, even if that person is your child, look very carefully. Search within and see if you know what is indeed in the other's best interest. Is your involvement interference, or guidance? How can one know the difference?

Parenting is one of the hardest situations in which to learn non-judgement. Letting go in parenting flies in the face of society. It challenges every value the world of form honors. But letting go in parenting also demonstrates that you trust God to oversee your child's welfare -- and who but God is better suited for such a role.

Part of the pain you now feel is that you must admit helplessness and powerlessness. You cannot "fix" a loved one, you cannot force him into filling the expectations you hold for him. But my child, when you are acting out of loyalty to ego, you ARE only helpless and powerless. Any power you ever felt while in ego was temporary, as was any help you ever extended through ego.

When you act from your heart, from the Divine Will which you share with your Father, then you ARE helpful and powerful, and more important, you can stay peaceful.

Stay above the battleground. See the drama from a distance. Deep within, everyone who is in this drama knows that all has already been corrected. The end of the play leads home to God for everyone. Even those who don't remember this truth are now faced with the opportunity to remember this truth.

The fears you now entertain are the same old fears. *"Will the rest of the world (family and friends) approve of me if I don't behave as they expect? Can I face the isolation and rejection of their disapproval?"*

151

The answer is -- yes, you can. The disapproval of the world is after all illusion, not real, part of the nightmare. God's approval is real and transforms the nightmare into the happy dream.

Use this opportunity to trust Me. Use this opportunity to teach others that trusting God is safer than trusting the ego. No guidance that comes from the world of form can bring any real joy. Your role is rather to stay out of God's way as He works with your brothers.

Let Me help you. I will give you the words to say when words are needed. If you are conflicted, return to Me and ask for peace -- do not ask what advice to give or what directions to deliver. Continue to extend love. Be a healer, not a judge.

Forgiveness is your function. Forgive anyone you see who is in pain or trouble, for they reflect your pain and troubled heart. Then forgive yourself for seeing that lack, for you already know that in reality, the brothers and yourself are already healed.

Challenges will come, the world will say you're crazy, insane! But the witnesses to God's Truth are also calling to you to see them. You will witness healing if you but look for it.

Trust, dear child. I will show you the way. Lean on Me, for My strength is yours when you are willing to accept it. We are healing the world, you and I . Your brother offers you healing. Accept it, then give it back to him, for to give is to receive.

TROUBLED TIMES

January 19, 1988

Daughter, do you see that the messages are prolific when you are troubled? What better, clearer evidence could you ask for to witness to the truth that what you perceive as "trouble" is merely opportunity to learn.

Someday you will see the opportunity to learn as just that -- opportunity, not trouble. Until then, I will help you find your way out of trouble and into the light.

You have chosen to allow the learning to escalate. At any moment you can choose to slow it down. But you cannot choose to stop the learning altogether.

Continue practicing gratitude, my dear. Continue practicing trust. Continue seeking truth. Continue serving My children by blessing them with your love.

DECLARE PEACE TODAY!

January 20, 1988

Withdraw from the war, and the battles will cease. Refuse to engage with the enemy and the enemy becomes neutral. You keep declaring the wars in spite of the pain the wars bring you. You engage out of old habit because you were taught as a child that warfare is inevitable, and that winning feels better than losing. Now you are being asked to shed an old habit pattern. Let go of war -- it is not peaceful! It is bad for you! Declare peace instead!

What is totally lacking in warfare, is communication. What will replace warfare in the new way of seeing, IS communication. Peacefilled, loving communication builds bridges to join, it does not destroy them to ensure separation.

"But," you say, *"What if only one brother will communicate. Can there be one-sided communication?"* Yes, dear one. For when you extend from your heart, it is received with the other's heart. Even though the other may deny the offering, it will be received when he is ready to accept it. When it seems that communication with words is dead, continue to communicate from your heart. Send love. Send only love. Do not be drawn into the battle.

This is not as difficult as you imagine. It is just difficult because old habits have been hard to break in your experience. But try to take one step at a time. Withdraw from the tiny skirmishes, then from the larger engagements, and finally from the open battle ground. Make small decisions for peace, one moment at a time. Ask for reinforcement from Me at every turn. Be watchful of the tiny doubts -- release them immediately. Move ahead slowly. Remember to include Me as your partner and together there can be only success.

Success, as you know, is peace. Peace for all. Declare peace today!

BE NOT SEPARATE
January 21, 1988

My dear, I realize you are in pain. I hear you think, *"if they would just leave me alone, I'd be all right. I'd be at peace."*

But, dear one, that is impossible. You can never be at peace alone, for you are One with your brothers and it is in the attempt to separate that you experience pain. Pain then grows more acute the more you try to build distance between you and your brothers. Focusing on the differences brings pain. Nurturing specialness brings pain. Trying to please one and not the other brings pain. Mistrust brings pain. Competition brings pain. Even losing and winning bring pain.

All these things bring pain because they deny your natural state which is Oneness. Therefore, the only acts/ thoughts which bring peace are the thoughts which support joining.

Because of your human learning, you think that to join with someone else you must give yourself to them, and to give means you have "given up" something and are lessened by the giving. Not so! To join with someone assures you of maintaining your wholeness. In fact, you do not experience your wholeness until you join.

Look to your past experience for the witnesses to this truth. Were not your most unhappy moments, the times when you felt isolated from everyone else? Whether you chose to isolate yourself (rejecting others) or whether you perceived that others withdrew from you (being rejected) the result was the same -- sadness, melancholy, sometimes despair.

Now look to the moments of happiness. Don't they always involve sharing, helping, being helped, cherishing and being cherished by another? So you see, my dear, your need to join, even in the conflicted ego state, is so overwhelming that it cannot, it Will not, be denied.

Therefore, ask not "to be left alone". Seek joining instead. Fear not that you will be diminished. Join with your holy brother in his/your heart. There it does not matter if you agree or disagree, if you share interests and hobbies, if he is rich enough, good looking enough, intelligent enough, popular enough, skilled enough, even "enlightened" enough. For in his heart, he is you, and you are him.

On the plane of ego, it seems difficult to let go of all the apparent differences. See beyond them and seek to join. My child, you need but be willing -- you do not need to achieve. I will facilitate the act of joining if you but ask Me to help you join from a place of willingness in your heart.

Are you willing, my child? Are you really willing? That means looking at everything in your life to see if it is meaningful or meaningless. Then be willing to release what is not meaningful. The only things/relationships/experiences which are meaningful, are those that contribute to joining. Being willing to join means being willing to sacrifice your investment in separateness. This is the one form of sacrifice which I can transform into holiness.

This is where the true work is, my dear. Not in performances, or good deeds, but in searching in the heart for the willingness to let go of all ego's hidden drives which bind you to separateness. Upon finding them, ask for My help to release them. Then you can join with the Sonship -- then salvation is yours and theirs. Peace.

ANGER

January 23, 1988

Anger is a personality trait you dislike, a personality trait you don't even allow in yourself. You consider yourself a patient person: kindly, benevolent, tolerant, and controlled. You are of a peaceful disposition and even see yourself as a peacemaker/keeper. Your placid demeanor sometimes borders on the dull, and no one ever saw you throw a temper tantrum!

And yet, dear one, anger is more a part of your ego self than you realize. It is not just something that exists "out there". Displays of anger in other people embarrass you and sometimes frighten you. And being the object (victim) of someone else's anger is extremely painful to you. You avoid other's anger scrupulously. By now you have learned that anything avoided passionately bears examination.

My dear, anger is a normal part of the ego state. It cannot be escaped. Indeed it must not be escaped. It must be recognized, experienced, and finally released. Anger must be addressed as part of the human condition, as part of the world of form.

The little girl you were, withheld displays of anger because she so feared the consequences. She imagined withdrawal of love was the result of expressing anger. So she buried the anger, disguised it, or denied it. Now it surfaces, because unacknowledged anger destroys the peace. It is now time to look at how anger was born in you, and what happened that it became repressed. Then you will be able to let it out into the Light.

My dear, all humans learn about anger and its repression very early. In the womb, the human experience is of "oneness". Even as newborns you felt whole, undifferentiated from the mother and the surroundings. The memory of "oneness" was still upon you. But as you grew, you perceived that the others were outside of you, and they were needed for your survival and happiness. You experienced hunger and discomfort and therefore lack. Others were needed to supply the lack. Wholeness ended -- conscious dependency was born. Fragmentation and separation entered. Ego's separation devices became strongly established in you, the small child.

For a time the little child still tried to hold on to "oneness". He risked loving openly, hungrily, and unabashedly. He even demanded his need to be loved be met. His feelings and needs were clearly expressed.

But eventually and inevitably, all human children experience rejection. And so did you. Through adult inattentiveness, or thoughtlessness, or deliberate negativity, the child felt excluded, even abandoned, alone. Parents, often unknowingly, withheld love in the name of discipline. The child, feeling rejected, withdrew into himself, deepening the separation.

The pain of having to support separateness was so great that the child could not escape anger. His secure world (which began in "oneness") dissolved, little by little, as separateness became his new playmate. He realized his total powerlessness, his total dependency. Anger then supported him -- justifiable anger. Rage and fear became his companions, his champions. His "oneness" stolen, fury descended.

But the child soon discovered that the anger he felt could not be openly expressed because it produced more distance between him and his loved ones. Too much separation is intolerable, threatening, and terrifying. So the child denied or repressed or postponed expressing his anger. That anger, unexpressed and unacknowledged, remained a tragic part of his bundle of human despair.

Some children found ways to experience and express

their anger and got on with the day to day strife of ordinary living. Some children pushed the anger so far away that they forgot about it. "Being good" seemed to serve in most child/adult confrontations, so "being good" replaced being honest about feelings.

You are one of the children who chose to "be good" to earn the ongoing love of your parents. And the "good" child that you were, you skillfully disposed of any anger that came along. And so your storehouse of unexpressed anger grew to overflowing.

Now, my dear, you -- the adult -- are finding out that facing the anger of others is just as painful to bear as was the original rejection you experienced in your childhood. You are beginning to remember the slights and misunderstandings, and powerlessness of being a child. You see that your whole life has been played with yourself cast in the role of "victim". Being the victim feels unjust, unfair and undeserved. For you are a "good girl" and have spent your life perfecting that role. So the pain you now feel, makes you angry!

Ah, so now the anger surfaces to be looked at, experienced, forgiven, and finally released. This is a necessary step in your unfoldment. Dealing with your anger cannot be avoided forever. It has arisen at this time because you are finally ready to deal with it, instead of to deny it. I have seen your willingness to let go of what is no longer of value, and your past anger is part of the letting go that will lighten your burden.

The process need not be devastating, nor even painful, my dear. Ask Me for help. Ask for correction in the conditions of your mind that gave rise to the anger. You need not touch each and every trigger point in memory. You need not experience them with the powerlessness of the child.

Now you can experience the anger as a conscious Son

of God, a Friend of Spirit, a Co-Creator with the Father, a Brother of the Christ. I can and will help uncover and bring to the light the old forgotten angers.

You ask, *"How do I get in touch with feelings so deeply buried that I am unaware of them? I am willing to do the work, but I don't know how to begin. Help me, Spirit."*

My child, to become aware of the old angers, become watchful. Look carefully at every irritation you feel. Be alert to each and every petty offense you experience. Notice when the people around you offend or insult you. Know when you're holding grievances. Behind these feelings is the memory of betrayal. Behind these feelings are the seeds that gave rise to rage and the original anger.

Notice how you "hold your tongue" when speaking to people who annoy you. Notice how you withdraw into silence when your impulse is to strike out. It is at these times that you need to ask for My help. Together we can move into the feelings and words that you withhold, and discover their cause deep inside, and then finally release them!

All that needs be done, is that you cease to deny your anger when it begins to surface. You need not act it out, but you must let it into your attention. When it is in your attention, I can help you deal with it as the adult who knows who she is, a loving Son of God.

That which is concealed cannot be healed. And that which is released to the light can only give rise to clarity and love. Come with Me now, and together we will heal the angry child within. The only anger that can hurt you is the anger that you keep hidden. When you let the old fears up you will discover that they are simply veils drawn in front of Truth. Lift the veils and the full Truth is revealed. In Truth, nothing is, nor has ever been hidden. That is what you will experience. And then you will be free.

Peace to you, my child. Remember, "All things are lessons God would have me learn." Some are not more difficult than others. They are all equally important, and unimportant! Invite Me into your every decision, into your every thought. Reclaim the "Oneness" that is your heart's desire. Peace.

"I LOVE YOU?"

January 24, 1988

My dear, your need to hear, "I love you," aloud is simply a smoke screen, a distraction to keep your mind from recognizing your one real need -- which is to hear yourself say, "I love you," to you.

Ego would have you think that what is wrong is that your loved ones do not support you, as demonstrated by their failure to say, "I love you," aloud. In truth, your loved ones demonstrate that they do love you through actions. Communication through acts is every bit as valid as communication through words. Indeed, if suddenly all your loved ones miraculously decided to shower you with open declarations of love, you would probably doubt their sincerity and ask that they "show you" rather than fill the air with empty words!

The real issue here is that the one who withholds love from you, is YOU, not them! The work therefore, requires your willingness to release all judgement about yourself, to look at and let go of self hate, self doubt, and self pity.

Whenever judgement of yourself arises, it betrays an unloving act directed toward you. Judgement of yourself is an attack upon you. Only ego attacks. Error, and lack, and sin, and mistakes exist only in ego's world, the world of separation.

In God's world, there is acceptance, total lack of expectation, absence of success and/or failure. In God's world, there is only love -- and love sees no lack, love sees only the whole.

Choose which existence you want to trust -- the world of judgement, or the world of love. If you choose to be in the world of love, you must recognize your own presence there, and love yourself.

Ask Me to help you rise out of self doubt, pity, and

condemnation. Accept My offering to you, which is repeated with every beat of your heart. "I love you." Yes, my child, I do love you with the Father's Love which knows no bounds or limits. With such love as this surrounding you, how could anyone, including yourself, fail to love you! You do not need to hear those words from anyone else. Accept them from Me.

When you have truly accepted My love, it will follow that you can say to yourself, " I now love myself. I love me."

All humans struggle with self hatred. (In fact you are more generous with your love to others, than you are to yourself.) Self hatred is the fuel which fires ego's power on earth. It is self doubt which assures the continuance of the separation. It is self pity which sustains ego as the self-declared god of the planet. But all humans will learn, in time, to love themselves. And that is the day that the kingdom of separation will be replaced by the Kingdom of the One.

Practice saying, "l love me." Practice receiving others' love as real. Practice letting go of self doubt and negativity at the moment it enters your mind. Turn over the error to Me and ask that your mind be healed. Only with My help, can this self torture be ended.

Accept that I love you. That is all you need. Then together we will return to the Source which is Love itself. Peace, my child.

LEARNING ABOUT LOVE

January 25, 1988

Human beings who don't love are in constant pain. Loving is the only real emotion humans can experience, and when they deny this to themselves by withholding love from self or others, they are choosing misery.

In the Course, you are learning that God is Love, Creation is Love, the One is Love, Reality is Love, You are Love, and your Brother is Love. That idea is so monumental that it makes you doubt your understanding about love, you become impotent, and therefore are unable to express or even receive love.

Just as there is only One Creator and many Co-Creators within the One; there is only One Love, with many expressions of Love within the One. That is why it seems that there are different kinds of love in the world of form. All love shares the same Source and therefore, all love is the expression of that One Source. But you humans must learn this bit by bit, by experiencing love from many perspectives.

Earth is the playground and schoolroom of love. In the world of form, your task is to learn about love and forgiveness. This is the only helpful learning available on this planet. That is why you are here. If you knew all about love, you wouldn't be in the world of form, you'd be in Heaven! No expression of love on earth is little. An no expression of love on earth is limited, if you use it to connect yourself to your Self!

Any thought which maintains or strengthens the idea that love is not real, is preserving the idea of "hell." To analyze love, chases it away. To reject love, delays your hapiness. To withhold love from yourself or brothers, causes the Son of God much pain. Rejecting any love experience or any opportunity to extend love, is a denial of your purpose on earth, and causes suffering. Forgiveness is just yourself inviting love's return after ego has denied it, or rejected it, or refused it entry.

So I say to you, shower yourself with love. Delight in all of its expressions. Accept every brother's attempts at expressing love, realizing that every attempt at loving is a holy lesson and pleases the Father.

Be generous about love: love good books, love learning, love music, love animals, love nature, love your work, love your play, love good food, love excitement, love silence, love sharing, love cerimony, love God's Word, love fun, love mystery, love beauty, love the known, love the unknown, love feeling good, love Yourself, and love Your Brother!

Be simple about love. Be fearless about love. Be expressive through love. That is all. Peace to you, loved one.

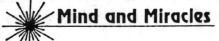 **Mind and Miracles**

16363 Cammi Lane
Fort Lauderdale, Florida 33326
(305) 389-8076